The First Few Wars
Are The Worst

His Grace Has No Measure

To Ken and Pam with much appreciation for your friendship and hospitality Jan

John F. Keith

*Oakville
February 22-24, 2000*

Canadian Baptist Ministries

Canadian Baptist Ministries
7135 Millcreek Drive
Mississauga, ON L5N 5R4
www.cbmin.org

Canadian Cataloguing in Publication Data

Keith, John F. (John Frederick), 1932-

The first few wars are the worst

ISBN: 1-894031-09-1

1. Keith, John F. (John Frederick), 1932-
2. Baptists -- Missions.
3. Missions, Canadian.
4. Missionaries -- Canada -- Biography.
I. Title.

BX6495.K45A3 1998   266'.6'092   C98-950161-2

Edited by Audrey Dorsch/Exchange Publishing
Printed in Canada by:
Gaspereau Press
P.O. Box 143, Wolfville, NS B0P 1X0
www.gaspereau.com

Lovingly dedicated to

Edith May (Gibb) Johnson

and

Rev. Gordon W. Johnson

Their attentive care of Mother Gibb from 1973 to 1997
permitted us to continue unimpeded in the international service
out of which experience these stories are written.

Table of Contents

Foreword

This volume is deliberately written to include a readership of men. Too often men have tended to step back from both interest and involvement in the world mission of the church, to everyone's loss, including their own. They have often considered it to be women's work, and have thought of it as less interesting than other fields of involvement that they considered more appropriate for men.

In the late 1950s or early 1960s a well-trained and competent woman, an ordained member of the clergy whom I knew personally, approached a village chief in western Congo. Her presentation included comments that she had an important message for him and his people. This was a message from God and from the churches of America. The chief's commentary (whether directly to the woman or only to others present I'm not sure) included words to this effect: "If the men of America had something important for us to hear they would have sent a man to tell us." Prejudices and stereotypes, however inappropriate, exist on all continents. Important tasks such as the commission to make disciples among all nations require the participation of both men and women. Certain avenues of ministry, service and communication are more open to women than to men, others are more open to men than to women. My goal has been to foster a balance. For that to be reached, the interest of more men must be awakened. For decades women serving overseas with Canadian Baptist Ministries (CBM) and other organizations have had the courage to be mechanics, builders, administrators and many other things in addition to another main assignment. They have done this under conditions that were and still are very difficult, often perilous. I pay high tribute to their readiness to undertake what no men were prepared to do.

Many men have expressed surprise at how interesting and challenging my career of forty years has been as I sought to serve my Lord internationally. Early in my career in Angola I discovered that my work was more than just interesting, more than just challenging. It was fearful. And one of the main themes I have set out to follow in this account is the process by which a fearful teenager was able to rise by the grace of God above constant fear, and grow into accepting challenges that were beyond natural ability or training.

An evening meeting took place in the early 1970s. New missionaries were being commissioned at Yorkminster Park Baptist Church in Toronto. Certain personal tensions were represented in the attendance that night, symbolic of struggles within the world mission of the church. The sanctuary is a large one and other churches of the city were well represented. Somewhere toward the front, perhaps in the tenth or twelfth row, sat a man with a small electronic device in his pocket; it was not a hearing aid. He had come prepared. It would be easy, at the sacred hour when the whistle blew to open the playoff game, to slip an inconspicuous earpiece into place. The fine grey cord extending across his blue suit to the transistor radio would never be noticed. He would restrain himself from shouting. The Stanley Cup playoffs were underway and the Maple Leafs had a game that night, a game that placed two sacred institutions in juxtaposition—sports and the missionary movement.

It would be quite unfair to suggest that the tensions pitted men against women. There were women definitely interested in sports and the fate of the Maple Leafs. There were men definitely interested in and firmly supportive of the missionary movement. But to an alarming degree, committed Christian men in Canadian society had for years been relegating "missions" to the women, often sending courageous women alone into the world's hard and dangerous places to do tasks that did not belong to women alone.

The meeting proceeded. Young people were commissioned for service abroad, and the level of interest ran high. At the end of the service a woman purposefully made her way to me through the crowd.

"Leland was so interested he didn't even tune in to the hockey game." This was something of a victory in her eyes. Chalk one up for missions. But that was only a battle won, not the war.

One of the unique components of that night's program was the key speaker. Not a North American, this prophetic voice had come to us from Peru. Samuel Escobar was Canadian director for Inter-Varsity Christian Fellowship at the time. He chose as his text *We have this treasure in earthen vessels"* (2 Corinthians 4:7). His thrust was that we must be protective of the treasure, not the vessel.

"Missionaries have often found it difficult to distinguish between the treasure and the vessel, they get to be protective of the wrong thing." Missionaries tend to be protective of themselves, their country and culture, even protective of the politics of their home country. When someone criticizes the country from which they have come, missionaries too often rise quickly in defence of their country's policies and politicians. The points Samuel Escobar made were entirely valid, and his admonitions precisely on target.

There has been a serious failure in communication. The process of fulfilling the world mission of the church is fully as interesting and as exciting as sports. That message has not been communicated adequately to men. Samuel Escobar did justice to a serious issue, and his presentation captivated both men and women. Missionary presentations over the years may not have been adequate in presenting the elements of drama, excitement and fulfilment for those personally involved. If so, a corrective element is needed.

So it is without apology that I set out to recount selected experiences and events that accompanied these forty or so years of international involvement in the mission of the church. The original goal in writing was to undertake the story of how Canadian Baptist Ministries made its transition, in the 1970s and 1980s, to a post-colonial style of relating to overseas churches. That still needs to be done. Hearing that I was to undertake some writing, a Baptist layman laid this challenge at my door. "John, I don't want this to be just another book like the ones I can pick up in church libraries. I want you to write the kind of book that shares the adventures. Something I won't be able to put down until I have finished it."

With that kind of intention, an obvious theme soon began to emerge. It was a focus on the grace of God, experienced again and again, often under circumstances that were difficult, or exciting or both. At first it was the more dramatic personal experiences that surfaced in the memory. Angola's war of independence began on a hillside behind our house. Our family served in Congo during that Republic's early turbulent years. Virginia and I were stoned in India, escaped shootouts in Kenya, and ministered through turbulent years in Yugoslavia, then Croatia. I experienced a hostage environment twice in Bolivia. Upon reflection, it became evident that God's quiet provisions and leadings that are unrelated to violence and danger should not be discounted. When seen through eyes of faith they carry their own dimension of excitement and drama.

It is most inappropriate to place missionaries on a pedestal, or even to hold them in any exaggerated or elevated esteem. In any event, it never happens overseas, where nationals and expatriates alike live too close to the realities for pedestals to survive. It could only happen in the "sending" countries. Many people I have met in Canada would insist that they do not worship missionaries, yet I suspect that they worship the *concept* of missionary—equally inappropriate. The world mission of the church is central to the very being of the church, and it will always involve people. The title "missionary" is not in itself a biblical word. It has been misused, abused and misrepresented, to the extent that the name may need to be abandoned in order to implement the tasks that are so vital.

Escobar's thrust was precisely on target. The great value, the treasure, consists of Jesus—who he is and what he offers. The missionary is only the vessel, the carrier, of negligible value. The challenge is to make sure that the value is placed in the right spot, and that we are defensive of the treasure, not the vessel.

John F. Keith
June 1998

Chronological Summary

1932	John Keith born July 13 at Corn Hill New Brunswick Public school education at Corn Hill and Sussex, New Brunswick

1950s

1950-1954	Gordon College, Boston, Massachusetts. Graduated, B.A. in theology
1954-1957	Gordon-Conwell Theological Seminary. Graduated, B.Div.
1955	Married Virginia Gibb June 11 at Wenham, Massachusetts
1956	Carol Esther born August 22 at Beverly, Massachusetts
1957	Appointed to service with CBFMB* Sailed New York to Lisbon, for language study and acculturation
1958	Shirley Elisabeth born September 18 at Lisbon, Portugal

1960s

1959 -1961	Angola
1961	Evacuation to Canada (Virginia in March, John in July)
1961	John Gordon born August 19 at Quincy, Massachusetts
1961-1962	Home assignment in Canada
1962-1966	Congo, founder-director of secondary school to include refugees
1966-1967	Deputation in Canada
1967-1969	Doctoral studies at Boston University Graduate School.
1969-1970	Return to Zaire for research and dissertation. Graduated, Ph.D. in anthropology

1970s

1970-1980	General secretary CBM office in Toronto, home at Burlington, Ontario, engaged in ministry, research and development of new ventures

1980s

1980-1990	Associate Secretary CBM, moved to Clear Lake, Ontario, travelling even more extensively

1990s

1990- 1996	Dubrovnik and Eastern Europe, several moves
1996 to present	Diplomatic liaison for CBM, based at Clear Lake

*Through a sequence of organizational changes since the 1950s, the following names refer to the same organization.

Canadian Baptist Foreign Mission Board (CBFMB)
Canadian Baptist Overseas Mission Board (CBOMB)
Canadian Baptist International Ministries (CBIM)
Canadian Baptist Ministries (CBM)

1
The dimensions of fear

I was lying on my side on a cement floor, my back tight against an outside wall of a brick house with a tile roof. Some two dozen students from our Bible school, with their children, were strung out along the various walls; head to feet, feet to feet, head to head, it didn't matter—just get against a wall and hold the little ones to comfort them. We had a reason for that position. If the heavy tile roof were to cave in under bombardment, the safest place would be along the carrying walls.

The angry roar of propeller aircraft engines passing at low altitude sent the little ones into bursts of crying again. We could hear both bombing and strafing. Bombs were falling in the valleys and forests outside the town. The strafing seemed to start at the bottom of the hill, proceeding upward toward us. The shooting became louder and louder until we could hear the double blasts—the explosions from the guns and the detonations on the ground. Close enough in fact, that we could feel the shock, but our shelter was never hit.

Inside, where we had gathered after breakfast for our morning routine of devotions and planning the day's activities, we listened, prayed, sang hymns, and tried to make sense of what we were hearing and experiencing.

Today that town is Mbanz' e Kongo, but in those days it was known as São Salvador do Congo. It was the colonial administrative seat for a district in what was then Portugal's overseas province of Angola. We were in the opening days of the struggle for independence.

What am I doing here? Looking back over a range of experiences on several continents, there are a number of situations when that question might well have been appropriate, though I don't remember asking it at the time. Probably I was too scared. One of them certainly would have been that morning in April of 1961.

The trauma of one's first three or four wars is the worst. After that we become accustomed to them to a degree; the panic and terror recede. But in those opening days of the Angolan war I must admit to a very real fear of which I am not proud. As people of faith we try to bring that faith into the stressful situations of life, to deal with the unknown, that which threatens, events that are utterly beyond our control. In the case of our family, the locations of our ministry repeatedly exposed us to hostilities. In retrospect we perceive that it is in situations of great trauma that our presence seems to have made the greatest difference to others. That being the case, there are lessons to be learned, insights to be shared that may have value to those experiencing stress of various kinds, not just related to violent conflict.

In October 1957 my wife Virginia and I, with our one-year-old daughter Carol, had gone with colleagues to Portugal for language study. Protestant missionaries were not really welcome in Portugal's overseas province of Angola, but were tolerated under certain conditions. One of those conditions was that our work be done in the Portuguese language. Another was that any institution such as ours must have a Portuguese national in residence on site.

Our arrival point in Angola in 1959 was Cabinda. From there we were invited to transfer to Calambata to head up the Calambata Bible Training Institute, which, besides administration, involved teaching classes for the twelve teacher-evangelists and their wives. We did this with a sense of urgency, as if to gain back the decades when such training had not been possible. More than a year in Portugal had ingrained an awareness of the heavy hand with which Portugal and its overseas provinces were governed. Secret police and paid informers were everywhere, with beatings, imprisonment and deportation of the native population being quite common. We concentrated on the task at hand, scarcely aware of the pace that political awareness was developing around us. We were certainly ignorant of the reality that we were living out the closing days of the colonial era, which in that part of Africa was more than four centuries old.

Virginia's mother, Esther Gibb, at her prayer station in 1990.

Signs of political change were there for the finding, but our eyes were not open to them. Sometime during 1960 a colleague had spoken about events in other African countries, implying clearly that a *Night of the long knives* still lay ahead for Angola. I remember standing under a full moon that reflected off the waxy fronds of the palm tree at the corner of our house. Inside, our two beautiful daughters were asleep, Carol a pre-schooler, Shirley just a toddler. I wanted so much for all four of us to survive. I was unable to see clearly past the survival issue to the issue of living in an enclosing shell of peace that could move with us and around us, whatever the circumstance. Not having faced or overcome the issue of fear myself, I did not discuss this; nor did I discuss the potential dangers with Virginia.

Our intense concentration on school and students may have intensified our shock and surprise when normal life ended overnight. History has it that the open hostilities in northern Angola began on March 15, 1961. Those of us living at Calambata, fifteen kilometres north of São Salvador, move that date one day earlier. There were disturbances but no deaths at Nsenge, where a government-operated mobile clinic was set up for the obligatory administration of pentamadine, used to control sleeping sickness. However, on that same day a Portuguese plantation owner was shot off his tractor by nationalist forces in the fields behind the compound where our houses and the Bible institute were located. Fernandes was on his way to see me, to return the wagon he had borrowed. He seems to have been the first casualty in that long conflict. The open hostilities that spread the following day across much of northern Angola eventually led to the establishment of Angola as an independent nation rather than a colony.

Bridges were blown up and roads closed. At Calambata, communication came and went only by road. We had no links with the outside world apart from news broadcasts received on battery-operated short-wave radio. We found ourselves in the middle of the war. That we actually survived unmolested did not endear us to the army convoy that made its way to Calambata after we had been four days in isolation. We were accused of having started or provoked the hostilities, otherwise how could we escape unscathed? Coffee plantations around us had been under attack. There had been deaths. We, the foreigners, must leave with the army convoy as they returned to their base in São Salvador.

The commander gave us a few minutes to gather together whatever few items we would take. We were still unaware that this was the end of our residence at Calambata. In fact, these were to be the closing days of the Angola segment of our lives. Because I refused to leave the student body behind, the student families were loaded on the back of local trucks commandeered from the population that accompanied the army vehicles. Canadian, British and Portuguese colleagues from the Institute travelled in our own vehicles.

From my childhood the Shepherd's psalm has been a familiar one.

. . . though I walk through the valley of the shadow of death
I will fear no evil, for Thou art with me . . .
(Psalm 23:4, KJV)

The whole point of this psalm has to do with being lifted above fear. The promise was there, but I missed its point because my focus was wrong. I was intent on survival, as if physical survival were the thrust of that promise, which it is not. The promise is that in passing through the dark and threatening valley, the one who is conscious of the Lord's accompanying presence can make the passage without fear of evil. The lifting of fear is one of God's great gifts, and its application is available for that entire range of human experiences through which we must thread our way. This lesson is not always learned early, and perhaps never learned easily. More than thirty-five years have passed since those initial frights in Angola when fear was so real that the very smell of it seemed to hang heavy in the air.

It was a few weeks after our evacuation to São Salvador that we endured the bombardment, huddled together against the walls of the room where we had been meeting. By this time Virginia and the children had been evacuated to Luanda; I had stayed behind with English and Scottish colleagues of the Baptist Missionary Society, principally to be with our Angolan student families. Over the coming months those students would make their way north through the forests to safety in the neighbouring Democratic Republic of the Congo.

Hostilities around our home began on March 14; my departure from Angola took place mid-July. So that first exposure to armed conflict lasted four months. In that period there was scarcely a night without some sounds of battle, often that staccato rattle of automatic arms.

In our time in Calambata I had innocently established personal links with a number of people who became combatants in the initial days of fighting. Like much of northern Angola at that time, the fields and forests around Calambata hosted herds of wild buffalo. Indigenous hunters were allowed only a kind of homemade muzzle loader, known locally as *canhangulo*. Colonial officials believed in gun control of anything that would be more threatening to their regime. The Portuguese invariably had a variety of firearms. Once, when I visited Ambrizete, a store owner invited me to go hunting with him. I learned that he hunted primarily on the game preserve, mostly at night, and from a jeep. His observation was that to hunt these vicious buffalo on foot was too dangerous.

Within the year I had purchased my own hunting rifle, a .375 Magnum made by Fabrique Nationale of Belgium. This gun easily carried the potential for hunting elephant, which also came to within a few kilometres of our rural home, but I had no intention of killing elephant. The Tsetse fly scourge where we lived prevented raising cattle. The painful bite of the Tsetse fly brought on sleeping sickness in humans, and killed the cattle. This resulted in a chronic shortage of meat. The nine or ten buffalo that I eventually shot were divided among teachers, staff, students, workmen, colleagues in São Salvador, and sometimes the villages along our road. My success in hunting brought a host of requests from local hunters to hunt with me. Among them were some who were soon to be militants in Angola's struggle for independence.

I had not foreseen the degree to which that rifle would bring acceptance among the village elders. Someone who could bring home a buffalo was a productive person after all, much more appreciated than one who only made marks on paper or blackboard.

Only years later did I learn of the courageous role played by two of our students behind the scenes. The rising of the population was not a spontaneous event. Former Angolans who had sought refuge in neighbouring Congo had been making preparations. When they judged the time was right, they sent messengers through the forests to alert local inhabitants, many of those being closely related to people planning the uprising. One of those messengers arrived in the student camp at our institute. João Matwawana and Henrique Josias went into the forest to negotiate for our lives. They argued that their teachers were not colonists, but were white people with a difference. We had not come, they said, to take land or to live off the population, but to bring assistance. To the courage of João and Henrique, and to God's grace, we owe our lives.

In a chance meeting in 1975 I was able to sit down and talk face to face with the messenger who had come to our Calambata forests to start the war, the very man with whom João and Henrique had negotiated our lives. I remember how remarkably dignified and quiet and statesman-like this little man was, in a plain navy suit without design. I began to understand him as someone deeply concerned about the future of his country and his people, rather than someone who had arranged a vendetta out of anger or revenge.

The army commander never knew the real reason we came unscathed through that first round of hostilities—and probably would not have understood the dynamics that protected one set of foreigners while revolting against another.

I learned something about a different dimension of fearlessness from a surprising source. Pedro Viera was short of stature, thin of frame, timid of appearance, and had a squeaky little voice that sounded even less significant than my own. Pedro became Virginia's assistant in the kitchen and around the house, freeing her to teach at the institute, and reducing the work load of a mother with two small children and no electricity, no running water, and no appliances except a kerosene refrigerator and a wood stove. Pedro was a self-styled cook, but whatever qualities go into making a gourmet, he possessed in negative quantities.

Whatever Pedro's shortcomings in the kitchen, he was fearless on the trail of a wounded buffalo. With nothing more than a machete he would charge into the elephant grass where visibility was only an arm's length. Pedro and I were in agreement that any wounded animal must be pursued unconditionally. This was not only to put the animal itself out of suffering, but to protect the women who travelled into the fields and forest planting their gardens.

The African buffalo is the most dangerous animal on that continent, largely because of its behaviour when wounded. It seeks out a quiet place for a day or two. The result is something like a person nursing a grudge and planning revenge. As the wound festers in tropical conditions the animal sets out in search of human scent, tracking down and goring anyone who crosses its path. At least one of our trips to the hospital in São Salvador was to take a man who had been gored by a buffalo. Stories abounded of men, women and children who were tracked down and often killed by enraged buffalo. The usual emergency treatment was to gather a handful of cobwebs from a thatched kitchen (where they were plentiful) and apply them directly to the wound, backed up by a handful of certain leaves. The medicinal use of herbs was fairly well advanced throughout much of Africa, Calambata no exception.

Pedro showed up more than once in a torn and tattered condition, his shirt shredded and his face scratched. Asked what the problem was, he would mutter, "*Aquela mulher!*" (That woman!) More than once I speculated that Pedro hoped to get wiped out in the glory of the hunt so that he would never have to face his little Maria again. I know from experience, however, that Pedro was not a fearful man on the hunt. Courage and

fearlessness may have a variety of components pushing them from behind.

After a hunt groups of hunters often came to admire the buffalo and to
run their hands over its hide. They were particularly interested in the
front shoulders, where the tough hide, perhaps as thick as 30mm, formed
a natural armour. When a buffalo charged it could be in a straight line
through thicket or forest. Its hide made the buffalo something like an
armour-plated vehicle when it charged through the forest, totally imper-
vious to thorns, snags, brambles and the ineffective shot from muzzle
loaders. Where a bulge in the hide indicated some foreign object, the
hunters would dig it out and discuss it. The bullet would not have pen-
etrated the full depth of the hide. The hide simply healed around it. (It
would be interesting to pass some of those old buffalo through a metal
detector.) Shot located, the hunting stories surfaced, much like hunting
stories the world over.

Whenever these innovative hunters located an old car battery they
melted down its lead plates and poured the molten lead into the green,
hollow branch of a papaya plant. Nature had provided this natural mould
that yielded a long, thin dowel of lead in the dimension they preferred.
The mould easily removed in an instant; the lead was chopped into seg-
ments; then each piece was patiently tapped into a sphere. The traditional style had been for hunters to work toward the centre of a vast
circle, dangerous as that may seem. As they closed in and the buffalo
eventually made a break for it they would try their shot, hoping to get
lucky. Perhaps not having grasped the significance of the power of my
rifle, they invited me to hunt in a circle with them. I agreed to hunt with
any of them, one man at a time, on condition that he remain beside me.

Looking back to those early days in Angola I am very conscious of
the grace of God that has carried me, often in the company of my family
and/or others, through a long series of events that could be, and often
were, disastrous. Nevertheless, significant ministries seem to have happened in the midst of that variety of violent settings. Our willingness to
continue in and through the traumatic situations seems to have opened
doors that would not otherwise be open to us.

This word *grace* refers to events or processes we experience that are better than we deserve. It is a word used meaningfully in the Bible to designate something God causes or allows, which we have not earned.

It was probably in the 1960s that *Amazing Grace* came to be popularized as bagpipe music. Previous to that, one phrase of it had already been ground into my consciousness by events in Angola.

> . . . *'tis grace has brought me safe thus far, and grace will lead me home.*

This struck me most forcefully at the August 1961 annual assembly of the United Baptist Convention of the Atlantic Provinces. The venue was the auditorium at Acadia University in Wolfville, Nova Scotia. The entire hymn was meaningful to me, and carried a depth of meaning that grew year by year. But when we came to sing these lines that day I dissolved in a wave of emotion. I was fresh home in Canada, having come through the first, and perhaps the scariest, of the wars that would dog our experience across a forty-year international career with Canadian Baptist Ministries.

"Safe" is a relative term, and "thus far" is an appropriate context for it. When are we ever safe? Bosnians who found themselves in so-called "safe havens" in their country during 1994 and 1995 still faced persecution, often torture and slaughter. They were declared safe, but safe they were not. Our own families in Canada and the United States often thought of us as being in dangerous Africa in those early days, and in various other danger spots since. They often welcomed us home to what they called safe North America. Yet it was while we lived on a quiet street in Burlington, Ontario, that the most harm occurred to any of our children. Son John had climbed 15 metres to rescue a kitten. His fall resulted in injuries that threatened at first to take his life and later to leave him totally incapacitated. Safety is not geographical; neither is it measured by those occasions on which God chooses to extend life rather than taking it. Matters of life and death are in his hands. We are safe with him, and safety is a factor of living in his good grace.

Not the least of the many different facets of God's grace in my life was the way in which God removed that dimension of fear that had ex-

A hay wagon scene at Corn Hill, early 1940.

pressed itself in so many forms, from childhood onward. If Mother were still living she would emphasize that my infancy and childhood were very active, perhaps even hyperactive, and always adventuresome. The fears were real but perhaps known mostly to myself.

The fear of new and unsure surroundings expressed itself the very first day of school. Any pre-school learning happened in the home, in the barn, in the fields, or at grandparents' home across the road from our farm in Corn Hill, in eastern New Brunswick. Then it was straight into grade one, some fifty days after my sixth birthday. I went to the first day of grade one crying and fearful, with one run back to the house for a toilet stop, then a second for some other excuse before the walk of one kilometre or so was inevitably forced on me. Fear of the unknown and the different plagued me. Fear of the big boys at school, a fear mostly unfounded, continued until about five years later when the bigger ones had all quit their attendance at the one-room country school, or had moved away from the community. There were other petty fears at school, too small and shameful to mention, but which still persevere in the mind.

Canadian children in today's schools would not understand my fear of disciplinary action. There is no question that physical punishment can

The Keith homestead at Corn Hill New Brunswick, 1943. Jack Keith with John, Shirley and Donald.

be an effective deterrent for children of my personality and disposition. The teacher would often take the strap from the desk drawer and place it on the corner of the desk as an encouragement to good behaviour. Some weeks would average two or three strappings, especially in those early years with lots of "big boys" still in school. Most of those older lads prided themselves that they could take ten smacks across the palm without shedding a tear or even flinching. Part of my fear was that I would disgrace myself by openly crying or even squirming and trying to escape. That I got through nine grades in that school without a strapping is not so much because I was good, but rather that I was afraid—and that I didn't get caught.

Fear of pain also explains my fear of the dentist's chair in that era before high speed drills. The only way past it was for Dad to carry me directly into the dentist's chair, and that without my full consent.

Mother and Dad did not fully understand fear of the dark; in fact they didn't seem to be afraid of the dark at all. To get to my bedroom in our

Ada Keith, teacher, in the doorway of the school at Corn Hill.

large farmhouse I had to cross a large storage room called the chamber—in the dark. The chamber had an assortment of trunks, boxes, dark corners and hiding places, various items for today's antique shops and a bearskin rug. Dad had shot the bear, and the mounted head featured a full snarl with all teeth showing except the eye tooth that cousin George had kicked out. Bedtime was always delayed three to five excuses past the appointed hour, but eventually I had to go up my private stairway to that part of the house, rushing across the chamber in the dark, slamming the door to my room, turning on the light and looking under the bed. If I had talked out these fears someone might have been able to help me, but part of fear is the fear of telling others about it. Churchill was clearly on target when he commented in that same era that we had nothing to fear except fear itself. There seemed to be no way of applying Churchill to my problem of getting across the chamber to my room at night.

Another dimension of fear showed up on the way home from my French and Latin tutoring in grade nine. I had to travel by bicycle to the next community for my weekly lessons. The return home was after dark, and I had to cycle past the cemetery. The legends and lore of a rural community emerge at community gatherings. Often enough I was one of very few young people there, and would often slip unobtrusively into the corner of some room where the yarn-spinners were taking turns at amazing and enthralling. At one of those events when I may have been no more than seven or eight, the focus of stories came round to cemeteries. The fine line between fact and fiction is irrelevant at such events, but a

Grandparents George and Lizzie Keith, with Donald, 1943.

little boy takes it all in. Joe had seen some kind of faint and pulsating green glow in the cemetery behind our community church. The telling of it was skilful in what he omitted and what he hinted at, as much as in what he said directly. There is a slight gradient on the road beside that cemetery that worked in my favour as I returned from French and Latin. I whipped through there at the highest speed I could muster, prickly hairs all standing on end at the back of my neck. Of course, once I got past the cemetery, the hill below the church took me nearly a half kilometre at top speed without touching a pedal.

These fears may well be assessed as common childhood fears, but I think I was more fearful than most. I saw myself as cowardly compared to my classmates and city cousins.

My transition out of fear to normal, healthy attitudes was not marked by any special signposts, except for one case: my fear of travel sickness. I wasn't actually afraid of flying, only of embarrassing myself yet another time by being airsick. I took my first flight at age 17, while working for the Bank of Montreal in Moncton, New Brunswick. My name was drawn to fly to Charlottetown for the surprise audit that habitually took place at each branch yearly. For me this was a big event and I was tense. The small plane crossed the Northumberland Straight, notorious

The Keith family in 1954, including John's sister Shirley and brother Donald.

for turbulence. Tension, rough air and a nervous stomach combined to produce the predictable airsickness. Nauseated on the way over and then on the way back, my batting average was one hundred percent, which set me up for trouble on any subsequent flights.

That unbroken record of travel sickness may have stretched through some thirty flights. It was a fearsome burden to live with, and highly embarrassing. The first sign of relief came on flights between Kinshasa, Zaire and Brussels, Belgium at the end of a week of sixteen-hour days spent preparing report cards for our Sona Bata High School. The report cards were designed by a bureaucratic school system to be so complicated that no student could figure them out, much less tamper with them. The form was only slightly more complicated than income tax reports. Any erasure or strikeover made a report card invalid; they had to be issued in perfect form for all 420 students, with dozens of entries on each card. It had been a demanding week, and we were headed for a time of relaxation in Europe, the flight funded by the Congolese school system. I got on the plane, fell asleep, forgot to be airsick, and had my first flight ever without that dreadful phenomenon.

On the return flight I began to understand that my airsickness was largely psychological. Far from relaxed at the end of this break, I was tense over the prospects of difficult tasks awaiting me back in Zaire. We got our family settled in their seats and I proceeded to ignore all subsequent events in the aircraft whether related to passengers, attendants' announcements or anything else. I also forgot that I had so recently come through a flight without nausea. Within twenty minutes I was predictably uncomfortable and began to dig out the convenience sack. Except, this time, I discovered that we were still on the tarmac. There had been a delay. We were still on the ground, stable, unmoving, yet I was airsick. Finally an awareness of my root problem began to sink in, and that was my road to recovery. I had not yet arrived, but I was well on the way, and it has led me to more comfortable flights.

In 1950 I experienced a year of transition from all that was secure and predictable to a new phase and style of life that for forty years would be characterized by risks, constant new beginnings, and dealing with the unknown. That long

Ada Keith said farewell to her only grandchild, Carol, at the farm in Corn Hill before John and Virginia left for Portugal and Angola.

journey began with an overnight train ride (sitting up) from Saint John, New Brunswick to Boston, Massachusetts to attend Gordon College. Facing costs in the vicinity of one thousand dollars a year, with no scholarship or family resources available, that journey began with $75 cash on hand and the willingness to work nights while studying days. By God's grace, the balance sheet at the end of seven years showed approximately the same cash balance, but with the additional assets of a wife (and her car), a child, and the two degrees that were part of our equipping for Christian ministry.

In the course of those seven years the level of insecurity about the new and the unknown was melting away quite unconsciously into new levels of faith and trust in the Lord's guidance and provision. But there still remained an intense fear of any occasion requiring that I speak in public. Through high school I had consciously used any options available to avoid all forms of public speaking, debate or class presentations. At Gordon College this fear began to surface as a serious impediment to my chosen vocation. Furthermore, aptitude tests revealed my distaste for personal contacts. When these were interpreted, a very wise lady took me aside and helped me to understand the issues.

John Keith and Bob Berry tenting at Fontaine NB during summer ministry, 1952.

"Looking at your tests I would conclude that you belong at Massachusetts Institute of Technology, not at Gordon. However, if your sense of God's calling is sufficiently strong, that will be enough in time to help you overcome your fear of public speaking and your distaste for personal interaction."

She was right. In a summer ministry of literature distribution in New Brunswick my partner Bob Berry and I sang and prayed our way through an encounter with some ruffians who had threatened to burn our tent around us. The fear of public speaking disappeared first with competent mastery of another language. The confidence gained in four years' exposure to daily use of Portuguese eventually contributed to a confidence when speaking in English. With a growing consciousness of how God had led me through a variety of situations, I was learning to trust him. I was also learning the valuable lesson of exercising silent prayer in moments of crisis and fear.

It was a gradual process. It was a work of the grace of God.

2
Portugal
Early lessons from a police state

Our residence in Portugal began in October 1957 and extended through to January 1959. This interlude in Portugal was required of all who hoped to work in the colony of Angola, known officially as Portugal's overseas province. The purpose included both language learning and acculturation to the Portuguese mentality, perspective and procedures. We were thirteen adults plus children, all serving with Canadian Baptist Ministries, all headed for Angola and all going through what is now recognized as culture shock. There was terrific mutual support in that company, with lots of fun and fellowship. I seem to have been the only one who came down with the Asiatic flu as we travelled on the Italian liner *Saturnia* from New York to Lisbon, which meant that I went ashore feet-first and horizontal.

We were living in the dying days of Portugal's forty-year totalitarian regime under which Salazar had exercised his benevolent dictatorship. By what appears to have been a coincidence, Virginia and I became eye-witnesses to the first of the bloodshed which, over the course of the next few years, would lead to a toppling of the regime. It happened this way.

Virginia's Uncle Fred and Aunt Edith MacKenzie were visiting from Kenilworth, New Jersey. Uncle Fred was the Brethren Assemblies' administrative approximation to a general secretary for their overseas mis-

John and Virginia with colleagues on the liner Saturnia from New York to Lisbon, October 1957.

sion work. A successful businessman, he performed this free and joyous service on a part-time basis. While in Lisbon en route to Angola for a field visit, they took us out for a meal. We chose a restaurant situated on a cliff overlooking the city square, where a political gathering or demonstration was in the making. That in itself was a sign of rapid social change in progress, for demonstrations had been unknown.

Portugal had four very active police-military organizations, their concerns being mostly internal, rather than about any threat from outside. Three of these forces were uniformed. The dreaded fourth was the PIDE, which operated secretly and mostly out of uniform. It was commonly known that the task of each force was to watch for any hint of disloyalty in the other three. To expose an indiscretion in any of the other forces led to a promotion in one's own. Among them they managed a very tight surveillance over their own nationals, but didn't overlook foreigners like

The Portuguese have long been a seafaring people.

us in the process. That night, in the square below us, one of those forces appeared in significant numbers, mounted on horses for crowd control. They began swinging sand-filled leather truncheons to dispel the crowd that had been gathering.

The police probably had no reason to expect that this night would be any different from the outcome of the timid years that had preceded, but in fact it introduced a different dimension. For decades nobody had dared to take a stand against the merciless iron fist of established authority. Wisecracks abounded on the street about how everyone in Portugal was willing to shed his last drop of blood for the *patria*, but nobody was ready to shed the first drop. It was shed that night. We stepped outside to the restaurant patio and watched a situation below us that was deteriorating rapidly.

At first the mounted police and their truncheons forced the crowd back, to a roar of voices that floated up to our level. Cobblestone streets provided this assembled horde with an abundant arsenal of square granite projectiles, slightly smaller than bricks, but heavier and more danger-

Lisbon wharf, from which Vasco de Gama and other explorers departed.

ous. The encounter between police and crowd rippled back and forth in waves. The stoning drove the horsed police backward; then it was their turn to respond with gunfire. There was no possibility that in this Lisbon of 1958 anyone except the police would be armed. In a battle of cobblestones against bullets the outcome was a foregone conclusion.

At the sound of automatic gunfire in the square, everyone in the streets of downtown Lisbon that night broke and ran. We could see streams of people running away in every direction. We ourselves did not stay to do a body count from our elevated position on the restaurant patio. Soon that spot, too, would become unsafe, and the police would not readily accept explanations of why foreigners were on the street at this critical time. Just by being there we would be under suspicion of being organizers and perpetrators. The place to be, from that moment onward, was indoors, with the shutters down.

No statistics of dead or wounded were ever released. The wounded dare not go to either clinic or hospital. It became unsafe to buy ointment or bandages at pharmacies, which all came under immediate scrutiny. Homes were searched for dead and wounded, no warrants required. Even the seriously wounded preferred to let lead poisoning, infection, gangrene and even death do their work in the secrecy of home or hiding place, rather than take a chance on discovery by the regime, which survived by beating, imprisoning, torturing and exiling any who might raise a voice. That week in Lisbon to be wounded was to be guilty, no trial needed or even considered. Voices had been raised—not even voices of protest—but they were quickly and violently silenced. Lisbon reverted immediately to its surface calm, with no evidence that anything would change.

Another visit that year was from a friend of Virginia's family, serving as a ship's purser. His visit highlighted the strict vigilance exercised by police. We already knew that authorities kept a close record of where each foreigner slept every night. The first week after we moved to our Lisbon apartment a policeman stepped out of the shadows, greeted us politely and unlocked our door for us with his key. Police activity tended to be polite, but definitely as firm as iron.

So when Jack Findlay came down the gangplank of his ship, looking for a public telephone to alert us of his arrival, he was met by a uniformed officer who asked politely where he was going. The officer instructed him to wait there for a moment while a phone call was made. He returned after no significant delay, instructing Jack to follow him. They both arrived at our door. The policeman followed Jack in as if it were the most normal thing on earth, and stayed to monitor all conversation. He shared in a meal at our table and eventually put Jack back on his ship. Jack, who was portly, white-haired and probably in his sixties at the time, was not the type who would appear particularly suspect of political or criminal activity. He was just getting the same treatment anyone else would get.

Virginia's parents visited family in Lisbon.

One Sunday evening I had gone to a worship service alone, Virginia staying at the apartment with our baby daughter Carol. Travel back from the service involved two or more streetcar rides and considerable distance. I allowed myself the luxury of a mindless trance, relaxing to the rattle and squeal of the trolley wheels and the gentle rocking motion that could put one to sleep if the seats had been more comfortable and carried fewer fleas. I came wide awake from this trance, suddenly alert that everyone was bailing out at top speed even though we weren't at a stop. I noted we were near the park at Marques de Pombal. A crowd was milling around, with those infamous police on horseback busy breaking heads with their truncheons.

Getting my bearings, I headed on foot up the hill toward the Largo do Rato, a stream of people running past me. Why should I run? I hadn't done anything, so I maintained a very brisk pace with as long steps as I could manage. The number passing me increased; the street was now full as well as the sidewalk, and the noise behind me was intensifying. I glanced back to see one cohort of the riders working this street, much nearer than before. They were swinging regularly at the nearest heads, not asking people if they were foreigners or if they were innocent. My own head would soon be a target so I broke into a run with the rest. The riders had us headed into the canyon, and the mentality was approaching "stampede."

At this point some of those in front of me headed for the open outer door of an apartment building, and I followed. A number of us, all unknown to each other, may have spent no more than ten minutes huddled under the wide stairway in the foyer, but it seemed like hours. The horsemen didn't bother with us, their task was to clear the streets. One could smell the intense fear by those who knew their country's regime. Consensus was that within the hour, and perhaps very soon, the teams of police, who always seemed to outnumber the population, would begin to work this area building by building, arresting any who were not registered as residents. Listings of all dwellers were complete and precise. I had to get out of there. By the grace of God I was able to find my way by small streets and alleys to our apartment.

We had been alerted from Angola that it would be easier to get our drivers' licences in Portugal. Once obtained in Lisbon it would be relatively simple to get a Luanda endorsement. We obtained a list specifying the eighteen documents and affidavits required for the valued pink document, which had lifetime validity. A few of the requirements such as photos, birth certificate and auto-school certification were predictable. Other items on the list approached the ridiculous. The licensing process was used as a catch-all to nab various sorts of offenders, ranging from bill-dodgers and draft evaders to dissidents, bigamists and criminals. Only a special, approved elite had the right to drive a vehicle.

It took a good part of three months to assemble this dossier, not a bad occupation during language study, for it provided lots of conversational

Decades after working together in Angola, the Keiths were reunited in Portugal with Luisa Machado, Sonia and Guilherme Neves, 1995.

interaction with officialdom. There were hours of sheer waiting in this line or that, often with instructions to return next Wednesday or on some other specified date, with additional required input. Documents were official and acceptable only when executed on official blue-lined paper of a certain format with the imprint of the state and a government watermark. Signatures had to be officially "recognized" and this alone was a formidable documentary process—our signatures are still on archive somewhere in Lisbon. Every official document required the appropriate value in government excise stamps. Sealing wax was required on certain documents, but not on all. All documentation must be painfully correct.

On the day I waited in line to present this impressive packet at the appropriate wicket I was convinced that finally all was in order as specified. Not so fast. The conversation was in Portuguese.

"You're missing the document verifying that you have *quarta classe*" (fourth grade).

"But I have copies here of two university diplomas."

"Those are foreign. How do we know they are equal to *quarta classe*?"

Portuguese nationals had a well-known prejudice in favour of their own superior educational system, convinced that it was unrivalled anywhere. Portugal's statistics of that era would certainly lend credence to that belief—if so few citizens attained it, it must be superior.

"How do I solve this problem—what can you accept?"

"A declaration from your embassy or consulate that you have the equivalent of *quarta classe*. I need it at my wicket here, but then it must be presented at that other wicket across the hall."

I could see that the wicket across the hall also had a long lineup. Between this wicket and that one across the hall it would need to travel back to the Canadian Embassy. Our departure for Angola by ship was already booked and time was running out. Even with the coveted document issued, would I have time to present it and get my licence?

"There is a way, by official bonded government courier. They can bypass the lineups, and a government courier could show it to both of us without needing to return to the embassy in between."

This was for a price, of course. The courier and I made our way by taxi to the consular office of the Canadian Embassy. I had phoned ahead giving the extensive details, and the document was actually ready when we arrived. To this day I consider the biggest documentary lapse of my career to be that I did not secure for my permanent enjoyment a copy of this precious document. It certified, on official Canadian government letterhead, that Reverend John Frederick Keith, (B.A., B.D.), has the equivalent of fourth grade. Our embassy there had learned to conform to local requirements such as full listing of my place and date of birth, plus full names of both parents, with Mother and Dad's own respective places and dates of birth mentioned, and of course my mother's maiden name.

And this process was recommended as being easier than getting drivers' licences in Angola.

These months of exposure to a police state and the Portuguese style bureaucracy made a heavy impact on the group of young Canadians headed for Angola. Nothing else could have prepared us so well for the colonial Africa of 1959, where severe measures of population control were still in effect, but fast approaching their end. The process would be dramatic.

3
Angola
Isolation and chaos

1959, the year of our move to the African continent, became for us a transitional year. It would be our last travel by ship, for jet engines and wide-bodied planes would soon become the norm. Our little family travelled from Lisbon to Cabinda, Angola on the freighter *Ambrizete*, four thousand tonnes. It proceeded first to Oporto to take on a load of wine casks. It also carried thirteen passengers. Those were an interesting two weeks, with sightings of porpoise and flying fish, and a stop at Las Palmas in the Canary Islands. Part of our activities involved guard duty on deck; otherwise Carol could have walked directly off into the sea at a number of places along the side where there was no railing. Shirley was still an infant.

Arriving in Cabinda's shallow bay, even this small freighter had to anchor offshore until we and our baggage were transferred to shore by lighter. Boarding the lighter from a ship's gangplank in a swell is an exercise in fine timing. Marilyn Taylor, one of our CBM group that had been together in Portugal, had a parallel experience at Soyo, on the other bank of the Congo river. She speaks movingly of the emotions that a young mother felt, handing her children from the gangplank to the up-lifted hands of the unknown people from another race who were offering their help.

The scene held lots of symbolism. During our years in Angola we were all surrounded by such uplifted hands. The people we had come to

The Keiths' first residence at Cabinda, Angola, shared with the Kimballs. A century-old Dutch trading company house, riddled with termites.

serve cared for us better than we would have been able to care for ourselves. Any hostility this contingent of Canadians experienced in Angola tended to come from the colonial administration, and even many individuals among those functionaries showed much friendliness. There was never a hint of hostility from the indigenous populations. Furthermore there were numerous friendships with Portuguese not involved in the administration.

At the outset of Angola's war in March 1961 two other Canadian colleagues were with us on site at Calambata. Dr. Walter and Winifred Johnson had come to study Kikongo with our English colleague Eileen Motley, appointed by the Baptist Missionary Society (BMS). Walter and I analysed the first signs of conflict as they emerged, not sharing them with Virginia, who was four months pregnant at the time. We wanted to spare her trauma, though of course she eventually had to face it anyway.

Anibal Machado, teacher at Calambata chats with John. The Keith residence in the background boasted no glass, no screens, no ceiling under the low tin roof.

The first hints that rang a bell with me had to do with a rush to buy salt at the small canteen run by our Portuguese Baptist residents, the Machado family, behind their house. It was primarily set up so that student families could get basic supplies, but village people from nearby were not turned away. A member of the Machado family would open shop every day in late afternoon. On March 14 there was a significant crowd of people, with a bit of pushing and shoving, mostly to buy salt—and in quantities! This was so unusual that it triggered memories of a colleague's comments that in one or two earlier conflicts with the Portuguese, local populations had started a run on salt in the stores. They were able to secure most basic supplies in one way or another under duress, but were dependent on Portuguese traders for salt.

These buyers were probably already well aware of two events that had taken place only hours before. Violence at the sleeping sickness clinic

The African "talking drum" was an advanced communication system even in the eighteenth century.

had sent the medical team scurrying. The nearby plantation owner had been shot off his tractor while coming to return a borrowed wagon. Such events were utterly unheard of, and certainly would lead to reprisals. Populations were preparing to abandon their villages, taking to the forest. Conflict was in the air. Walter and I could smell it.

Virginia's first recollection of something suspicious was when I insisted on accompanying her on that evening visit out back where we had built the beautiful, circular, brick biffy to surround and protect the twenty-five-foot "long drop" we had dug to the amazement of the countryside. (There is a theory that flies do not go below a depth of six metres, but I think we disproved that quite effectively).

By the next morning we were clearly in isolation, if not under siege. There was no morning bus from São Salvador. Someone had left a note on a forked stick in front of our Bible school classroom indicating that we were safe on this property if we did not leave it and did not receive people from outside. That would have been the impossible condition to accept, as we would not and could not have refused refuge to whoever came. However, that part was not tested.

The next four days of isolation had a weird aura of surrealism. Obviously bridges had been destroyed. Anibal Machado was loud in affirming that this was the equivalent of a brush fire that would be quickly stamped out. Our best source of information on what was happening in our immediate vicinity proved to be the BBC World Service. The habit, especially on over-

The Keith family as evacuated from Calambata, Angola, 1961.

seas assignments, of keeping a short-wave radio on hand and listening to the BBC six a.m. news became part of the routine of life that lasted until our return from overseas service at the end of 1995.

For this segment I draw as well on Virginia's recollections of her closing days in Angola, and of the tensions that we could sense immediately at Calambata. For openers, there was no more contact with the nearby village of Luanika. Viegas, master of the charcoal iron in our household, did not show up for work. Nor did the workmen who were building houses in a new village for student families. We lived in a hushed aura; it seemed as if the normal sounds of life had been muted. It was a time of intense prayer for guidance, safety, our student families, the future of our work, our school and Angola itself.

Tension increased as a platoon of ragtag marching men made its way around the bend of the road from Luanika, headed toward our house.

They carried muzzle-loading rifles and machetes, but were not accompanied by dogs—so it was not a hunting party. The road passed so close behind our house that we were able to see facial expressions, although they did not turn to look at us or give any signal of recognition or normal greeting. We gathered our pre-school daughters to us under the Mango tree, not at all sure what was coming. The cluster of men, probably a dozen or more, pressed forward, intent on some mission. This period of silent unreality when we were in limbo lasted four days. They were long days and long nights.

There are events we can chuckle about in retrospect that did not seem at all funny at the time. The Machado family had a standing order for bread with the bakery in São Salvador, and an arrangement with relatives there who would bag it and put it on the bus. The bus driver would toss it from his window at our compound. The phrase from the Lord's prayer, "Give us this day our daily bread" was taken so seriously that I once heard Anibal Machado give a morning devotional using an illustration that it would not be possible to live without daily bread (of the wheat variety). It may have been the morning of the third day of isolation that we heard the angry hum of a Dornier light aircraft engine. It came in low over our houses and began to circle the compound in a number of passes. We, the Machados, the Walter Johnsons and Eileen Motley all ran out and clustered by the Mango tree. On one of these passes the motor was cut back and, just as the plane approached again, something came hurtling down. It takes only seconds for that fall of perhaps one hundred and fifty metres. What went through my mind was "explosive," for we did not know the plane, or who might be in it. We gathered the children quickly, but it was Anibal who recognized his bread bag and ran to get it. Their relatives in São Salvador were alive, and had remembered them.

On the fourth day we heard the sounds of an army convoy in the distance. We heard the roar of trucks long before we saw the vehicles. Later we learned that the interruptions we noticed in the sounds of their approach represented the time it took them to build bridges over some small streams. They carried beams and planks with them for that purpose, as all bridges had been destroyed.

When they drove into our compound they were angry. Why should these foreigners be alive, safe and unmolested when Portuguese plantations along the same road had been attacked, some of their inhabitants killed? We must leave, they said. It was a military imperative. I refused categorically to leave the student families behind, so the commander compromised. The twelve student families would also be evacuated with us, on the commercial trucks that had been commandeered to accompany them and carry the bridging timbers. The convoy would go on past Luanika to visit one additional plantation, and would return to collect us. We must be ready within the half-hour.

The drive from Calambata to São Salvador was never fast, due to the condition of the dirt roads. On that day the fifteen-kilometre trip must have taken about five hours. Our two mission vehicles were inserted into the even slower convoy, which needed to rebuild bridges across two rivers and some streams. It was from the forests along the banks of these rivers and streams that the soldiers expected attacks on the convoy. A routine developed as we arrived at each crossing. They raked the forest with automatic fire, and tossed grenades (for these we had to lie down flat). Then they constructed a bridge, dismantling it and collecting the planks and beams after we had crossed. This was totally new to all of us, including the army itself. Children were terrified; the troops were jittery. For months afterward when our daughters saw violence on television back in Canada they would run from the room, or run at the sight of a bushy black beard. The convoy commander was bearded.

In São Salvador we were received and cared for at the compound of our close colleagues of the BMS. This is the historic Baptist Missionary Society of Great Britain, dating back to the sponsoring of William Carey. We were about sixty evacuees from Calambata, including institute staff and student families. The missionary and Portuguese women and children were invited to prepare for evacuation the following day. The BMS compound was to be my base of operations for the next four months.

The largest aircraft to land on the dirt strip serving São Salvador was the Beechcraft, carrying six passengers. An airlift of small craft was ferrying evacuees to the airstrip at Toto where they would be taken on to Luanda by cargo plane. The scene at both airfields was disorder, and

John Keith and João Matwawana in the 1960s with Manuel Senguele and Andre Conga da Costa, who were also students at Calambata, Angola.

emotions were running high. So was nationalism. At the São Salvador strip coarse field grass that we called elephant grass, grew right up to the edge of the strip. Someone fired a shot from the grass. We will never know whether it represented any serious threat or not, but in a setting prone to panic, with many on hand who had seen spouses killed before their eyes, it was interpreted as an attack on the airstrip. Everyone was ordered down flat. Virginia and our little daughters, in their matching mother and daughter dresses Virginia had made, stretched out in the dust.

There were bursts of automatic fire along the edge of the airstrip before boarding proceeded, then an intense rush for the plane, which put in jeopardy the passenger lists that had been drawn up. Pushing and shoving took over, with derogatory remarks about foreigners "who probably started all this anyway." Virginia and the children did not get on their designated flight; neither did Roma Shields, wife of BMS surgeon Dr. Roger Shields, and her daughter, or other women from the BMS compound. I suspect that some of the onlookers may not have considered me gracious when the plane arrived the next time around, but one way or another our people were flown out.

On to Toto then, where the potential for disorder was still greater, with a larger airstrip and with plantation survivors being flown in from a variety of smaller strips. Virginia and Roma Shields with the children found themselves on the back of one of those large army trucks that stand so high off the ground. At the other end of the strip a plane was loading for Luanda. There was no driver for this truck, loaded exclusively with women and children.

The front room of the Keith residence at Cabinda, Angola became a classroom for the Bible Institute.

"Virginia, you know how to drive," said Luisa Machado. "Take us over there." Virginia was four months pregnant, and with the crowding, she had to climb over the rack to make her way to the cab, which was totally unfamiliar. She had never driven a heavy truck. She describes having ground the gears until she found the appropriate combination and got her passengers to the plane.

Boarding, the passengers found no seats or seat belts, so they sat on their suitcases along the sides of the cargo plane. On the run down the airstrip one of the windows fell out, which involved a stop, a search for the window, a reinstallation. In Luanda some system was in place to farm out the arriving refugees to various homes and residences. Virginia, who was still an American citizen at that time, went with our girls to the home of the American vice-consul. Anti-American sentiment was running strong in the colonial capital, and the vice-consul's car was pushed into the bay. None of this added to her peace of mind. To top it all, during the three weeks that she stayed in Luanda no communication was possible with São Salvador. It was during that period that we in São Salvador lived through the bombardment that came so close without actually hitting us. She didn't know whether I was dead or alive, and she was unable to consult with me before being evacuated, via Paris and New York, to Boston where her parents lived. I arrived in Luanda one day too late; she had already flown to Paris.

Two occurrences in the Luanda airport shed light on what was happening across the north of Angola. The first had to do with the use of archaic Anson aircraft for bombing villages. In this the colonial army was using the civilian airstrip, the same one commercial flights were using for arrivals and departures. It seems the bombs were stored in a warehouse at the airport. As reported by a Portuguese civilian, the army was using small bombs, packed in around the feet of the man in the second seat. Over a village he manhandled these out the window. Even antique methods such as these represented ultimate weapons when opposed by no more than machetes and muzzle loaders.

I saw one Anson aircraft roar down the runway, obviously overloaded, unable to lift off. The plane braked to a halt and taxied to the hangar to remove some overload of bombs; then it was outbound again, barely successful in its liftoff. This was clearly hazardous procedure for a commercial runway still handling passenger flights, but they were considered to be extraordinary times.

In a second incident at the airport I sat close enough to listen to two pilots conversing. This was loud-mouthed talk which, in that era, they probably would have wanted any nearby foreigners like me to hear. The emphasis was *"Angola é nossa"*—Angola is ours and we have both the will and the ability to hold it. One pilot boasted of how many thousands of "them" had been liquidated by bombing on that day, the first Sunday after hostilities began. At the moment I didn't grasp the full significance of what I was hearing. Later the reports began to come in of church congregations being bombed in the central area of Angola where the Methodist mission worked. This would be before worshippers had received word of hostilities farther north. They would have had no reason to suspect that their lives were in peril.

It is unclear what planes or personnel of the Portuguese Air Force would have been in Angola at the outset of hostilities, if indeed any. However, there were two Portuguese national airlines, closely connected, and their pilots performed military as well as commercial functions while carrying civilians in their planes. I experienced this first hand when I returned from Luanda to São Salvador. The international line was TAP, the local one handling internal flights was DTA (something like Department of Air Transport) and theirs was the flight to São Salvador, by Beechcraft. Once away from the city one of the two pilots reached back for his automatic rifle and laid it across his lap. As we approached the combat zone our plane would circle major villages, now supposedly abandoned, to see if there was any sign of life. I missed a lot of detail by being such a bad flyer and troubled with nausea to a violent degree. I distinctly remember this co-pilot propping open, ever so slightly, the door beside him. He held the weapon in a firing position at the ready, in case movement were spotted in the village. No signs of life were seen on this flight, at least nothing that he shot at. I do recollect one wild buffalo in panic humping over a hilltop, for we were so close to the ground. Several times that day the pilot stood his Beechcraft on a wingtip, in a tight circle over a village. We were doing reconnaissance for the Portuguese army and my ticket was helping to pay the tab.

My source of stories was often the civilian population, the traders who ran shops in São Salvador. They loved to laugh at the ongoing feud between this DTA Beechcraft and an old African hunter in one of the villages who had managed to get himself a buffalo gun, against all the colonial government rules. The hunter had found himself a rocky outcrop where he could hide under a large flat rock, his flank protected by other boulders. When the commercial flight came over he would slip out to take a shot at the plane, then go to ground before their reprisals could get him. He was reported to have holed the wing of a plane, but never to have done more serious damage. Incidents like this are probably behind the life insurance caveats about travel in war zones.

To get on that flight back to São Salvador had not been an easy task. After a couple of unsuccessful attempts by phone to make bookings I took a more direct approach. Going to the DTA office in Luanda, I asked for the director.

"Yes, I know your flights are full but I'd like you to take someone off and put me on."

I was armed with the fresh memory of how Virginia, the children and others were bumped off the established evacuation lists from São Salvador. I admit with some shame that I still carried anger over that one, together with a sense of frustration at having missed contact with my wife before she left Angola. It appears that the director was genuinely ignorant of his pilots' private initiatives involving passenger lists.

"Sir, we honour our reservations lists, and we do not make exceptions."

I proceeded to inform the director of the exceptions I knew, giving date and place. I left my phone contact number and went back to my lodging, where I got a phone call informing me that I was booked on tomorrow's flight. I learned later with some regret that the pilot had lost one stripe and had taken a cut in pay. It was not my purpose to be vengeful, only to get on the flight.

Back at São Salvador life became more and more difficult for the students who remained behind. Those who were known locally had realized that it was too dangerous for them and their local relatives, so they had fled through the forest to Zaire. With those who remained we tried to maintain some semblance of ordinary life. Daily activities included morning worship, with hymns, music, prayer and a meditation. We attempted from time to time to continue some classroom work, if only to keep us occupied, but the studies were halfhearted at best. At least we spent regular time together.

Soldiers would walk by the BMS property where we were staying, look over the wall and make derogatory and threatening remarks to those who remained behind. "We'll get you one of these nights," was a favourite. Our situation turned a corner on the day the authorities came to search the students' quarters. They found a small radio in Salomão's possession. That was enough to prove his guilt—"Why would you need a radio?" He was taken prisoner and remained in prison throughout the remainder of my time in Angola. That event spooked the rest of the student body. The time had come for their flight as well.

In Paris, Virginia had encountered the straw that broke the camel's back emotionally. In the haste of evacuation from Calambata our health cards had been left behind. She and the girls were given yellow fever shots in Luanda, to permit them to travel. Officials at the Paris airport began to insist on other immunizations, but before they

Pedro Vieira, faithful helper and fearless buffalo hunter.

could receive them she and the children would need to be quarantined for an additional ten days. This threat of having to hold over for ten days in Paris with no money and only tropical clothing was too much. Always a calm person by nature, Virginia had shown great strength throughout, with no tears and no panic. But at this information she simply dissolved in tears.

They eventually worked out an affidavit from the American Hospital in Paris and she was able to proceed to New York and Boston, but not before a walk on the Champs Elysées with the children. For someone who had taught French and French literature at college level that was a minimal requirement when passing through Paris for the first time.

Back in São Salvador, the first thing I did after the women and children got away safely was to disassemble my hunting rifle, the powerful .375 Magnum that had kept us provided with buffalo meat, and which I had kept close at hand on the evacuation convoy from Calambata. I didn't want to use it for my own protection and I was equally adamant that it not be confiscated for use against the population.

On Palm Sunday, March 26, I was asked to speak at the morning worship service in São Salvador. This was just twelve days after the beginning of conflict, and my family had been evacuated. I prepared and delivered my message in Portuguese, and a translator relayed it in Kikongo. By the grace of God this language arrangement appears to have prevented a massacre on this specific day when massacres in churches farther south claimed many lives. My biblical text, relevant to Palm Sunday, was about Jesus' triumphal ride into Jerusalem on a donkey.

The church was packed, and the sermon was·just getting underway when several army vehicles roared into the churchyard at high speed, soldiers jumping out to take up positions at the windows and doors of the stone construction. Church construction in the tropics does not require glass in the windows. The shutters are open during services, to provide better circulation of air. Built at chest level, such windows make it comfortable for an overflow audience, standing outside, to see and hear through the windows. The soldiers quickly mounted their automatic weapons in these window openings, pointing inward. An officer came to stand in one of the doors behind the pulpit; armed troops blocked the other three doors. Never again would I have such a captive audience, I suppose, but my mind was not on puns. It was a fearful moment.

There may have been several courses of action to take at that time. I was preaching; we were still alive; the soldiers at the window were able to understand all that I was saying, so I simply continued. Never have I sensed stronger evidence of God's strength and guidance. I did no political or strategic analysis at the moment, I simply continued. Analysis later highlighted how unusual it was to have a sermon in Portuguese from this pulpit. The officer would have known that sermons were habitually delivered in Kikongo. He would have planned his order to open fire, and if he were ever asked for a justification for the order it would be that this was a political rally, fomenting uprising. Given the political climate of the day, that would have been sufficient. The problem, as it turned out, was that his soldiers could all understand precisely what was being said. There were too many witnesses among his own that this sermon carried no note of political foment.

Having surrounded the church in such dramatic fashion, how does one back off? That was not my problem, and the officer must have taken nearly a half hour to work it through. The next move was his. It's surprising, really, that so much of the sermon intervened before he took action. He came in and sat down on the edge of the platform facing the congregation, with his automatic weapon across his lap in a non-threatening position.

"You may have wondered what was going on." (We had indeed.)

"I don't want any of you to be afraid. We had heard rumours that there were people smoking "pot," (he called it *chanvre*) so we thought we'd come by and check. My men will check you on the way out. That's all."

Along the northern coastal area of Angola where Canadian Baptists worked there was a tradition established even before Canadians arrived, that church members were not users of tobacco in any form. That differed from the practice prevailing in the area served by the BMS. Many of their church members carried small containers of finely ground tobacco, a snuff that they inhaled. When the congregation filed out that morning (without a proper benediction it seems) there was a vast assortment of snuff bottles left on the floor under their benches, which might well have financed the operation for some time. The soldiers didn't even bother looking at the snuff bottles. There was never any real suspicion of drugs; the pretense of drugs was just their excuse.

Two or three events that took place during my four months at São Salvador may be worth relating. One of these was the attack on São Salvador. The buildup had been taking place in nearby forests for more than a week. São Salvador was situated on a hill, three sides of which were very steep and difficult to climb. The BMS mission property sprawled across much of the area where the only gradual slope of land led up to the business and administrative sectors of the town. We at the mission had two sources of information: those who spoke with us in Portuguese, and those who spoke Kikongo. These two linguistic groups represented the opposing sides in the conflict. Both agreed that a buildup of personnel had been taking place in the forests below the hill, and that an attack was now imminent. The most logical approach for an attack was across mission property.

What some would term the "native quarter" of São Salvador was already empty. The thatched roofs had been torched by the army. We missionaries had been called on the carpet, accused of resisting the burning. Dr. Roger Shields of the BMS was actually in prison over the affair. Most of that quarter's inhabitants had fled to the forest or to the Democratic Republic of Congo. A few slept at the army barracks with the Portuguese population; a few who had close ties to the BMS slept on the mission compound, a reluctant arrangement as far as the army and administration were concerned. This was allowed to continue on condition that BMS missionary Jim Grenfell or I physically lock them in the school at dusk and not open the door before dawn.

Jim and I had moved to his house, not appreciating the camping conditions required if we were to continue to sleep in the school, as the army commander had ordered us to do. We had steadfastly resisted his order to sleep in the army barracks. So now the city was surrounded, and rumour had it that the attack would be tonight.

There are many motivations for prayer, in general. The highest is adoration, worship, praise and gratitude to God. Ranking somewhere below this plateau is the desire to intercede on behalf of others who are in need. Lower again comes personal need and then, lowest of all, that old prayer lever, fear, which always seems to pry people out of their holes of spiritual complacency and neglect. I recall a deliberate effort to live entirely above fear, but I don't remember being that successful about it.

We prayed, I prayed, and for two nights the answer to those prayers came in the form of torrential rains. No attack developed. The third night was memorable for its utterly clear sky and lack of moonlight. There is a conflict at times between faith and doubt. That night I had serious doubt that I would be alive in the morning, that I would live to see my family again. We were told that the timing of the attack had been chosen deliberately to favour the dark phase of the moon. The stars were ever so bright that night, and this would indeed be the night of the attack.

Jim Grenfell and I shared a room with twin beds. A large, low and wide window between the beds had been designed for maximum air circulation. That window was only screened, with no thought to the kind of shelter or security one might hope for in a fire fight. Random shots had become the norm, every night of the week, and we had grown accustomed to sleeping with them. When the attack came there was no question of what was happening, and sure enough, it was on our side of the hill. I rolled off my bed, toward a wall, Jim did the same from his bed, toward the other wall. Our communications were by whisper, as we compared notes on the progress of the battle.

Those shooting muzzle loaders were obviously being pushed back toward the mission (they had gone up across it silently). The battle soon focused in and around the mission compound. Was the automatic fire from the verandah of this very house, just outside our window, or was it in our back yard? We fully expected that at any moment someone would break into the house, into the room where we were sleeping. Gradually the heat of battle pushed past the house on both sides, tapered off and eventually petered out entirely. Dawn was coming and with it came the full realization that we were alive, that by God's grace we had been spared.

There were episodes of high drama at Ambrizete, Quimpondo and Mboca, where other Canadian Baptist families were living who had been with us in Lisbon. No lives were lost from among these colleagues, but some of their stories are more dramatic than my own experiences. Weeks later, Bob Malcolm and I met and travelled together to Ambrizete, to assess the situation and to secure, if possible, vital items like documentation of property ownership. Arriving there, we were faced with an immediate decision about where we would sleep. The Mambu Mampa mission compound had been sacked and pillaged by the army or marines, and in any event the authorities would not have allowed us to be at the mission compound alone at night.

The recommended solution was for us to sleep at Nogueira's warehouse, where the army and most Portuguese civilians gathered each evening for their night's vigil, and to sleep if possible. Tiles had been torn up from a corner of the roof and a machine gun platform installed there, behind sandbags, to fend off any potential attack. There were also sandbagged bunkers at sidewalk level. Bob knew the man who ran a snack bar and a small hotel with a few rooms at the main intersection in Ambrizete. We asked his advice.

"You can do as you want, but personally I'm not going down to sleep among the fleas and bedbugs in Nogueira's warehouse, I'm going to sleep right here."

Not being fans of fleas and bedbugs ourselves we decided to stay there with him. Bob and I shared a small room with two beds on the north side, facing the main cross street that led down to Nogueira's. If there happened to be action that night, we would probably have a glimpse of it. In times of war where solid intelligence is lacking (and the pun is intentional), rumours replace dependable information. Rumour had it that a band of militants was on the coastal plain somewhere just south of Ambrizete. Bob and I discounted that rumour, and settled in for a night's rest.

What happened after one in the morning we are calling the attack on Ambrizete, tongue in cheek. For one unfortunate woman it was certainly a terrifying experience. We awoke to assorted gunfire, and got up with hearts thumping to peer out on the lighted street, which was just one level below our window. Firing continued; then shadowy forms appeared, slipping along from one sandbagged outpost to the next, defenders moving from Nogueira's warehouse toward the edge of town. They fired volleys from time to time, but we heard no return fire. I admit to wondering whether we may have made the wrong decision in staying at the hotel. In time the shooting died down and before too long it ceased completely. We went back to bed and probably to sleep, without news.

In the morning we were given a rundown on the event. A woman had gone into labour, and had headed toward a clinic near the village centre, assuming that she would be safe if she stayed in the open, and if someone accompanied her swinging a kerosene lantern. In normal times she would have been fine, but given the high state of tension all signs were interpreted in the worst light. It is my understanding that this poor woman, who came under a barrage of shooting, delivered her child on the spot. During later years I began to pay special attention to Kikongo names, especially those assigned when births took place during special circumstances. I suspect that this baby's name would reflect something of the occasion.

Virginia was in Boston with her parents, our third child due in late August. With the student body safely away from São Salvador, it was now feasible for me to leave, so that departure target was set for mid-July. Before going I had to do my best to see if Salomão could be released. In this case prayer, without making some serious attempt, seemed inadequate. At least I wanted to visit him before leaving, so I combined that effort with my leave-taking of the officials. There is a formula when saying goodbye, and the officials both used it.

First I went to the administrative secretary, paid my respects and said farewell.

"If ever there is anything I can do for you. . . ." He affirmed that he was always at my disposal.

"Probably not, but thank you," I replied. Then, "Oh, by the way, would it be possible to visit my student Salomão in prison?" This created something of an embarrassment in light of the affirmation he had just made.

"If he were my prisoner I'd let you, but he's the governor's prisoner."

It is just possible that I would otherwise have left without saying farewell to the governor, whom I had found less pleasant to deal with than the secretary. But I walked over to his palace. The governor was friendly enough that day, probably glad to see me on the way out.

"If there's ever anything I can do for you. . . ."

It's really not expected that one attempt to cash in immediately on such an affirmation—actually it's very bad form and quite unfair to the niceties of a civilized people. However, there was a lot in this war that I had found to be unfair, and the handling of Salomão had certainly been unfair. So I came back with my casual question.

"By the way, could I visit my student Salomão?"

Was I surprised by the answer? I couldn't believe my good fortune.

"If he were my prisoner I'd let you, but he's the secretary's prisoner."

When I walked back into the secretary's office it was with the warmest and most innocent smile I could muster under the circumstances.

"I have good news. The governor says Salomão is not his prisoner. Do you suppose he could be set free?"

That question was met with no enthusiasm at all, not even a hint of warmth. One might even say that the secretary was a bit frosty, but he did agree to take me to visit a very subdued Salomão. His face, and especially his forehead, bore scars from his beatings. His lips were chapped, like someone recovering from a high fever, but he was alive. I asked for the privilege of praying for Salomão. At that point the secretary moved into a position between me and my student. I closed my eyes as I prayed, but I have no proof that the secretary closed his. He was probably wondering if I would try to pass something to Salomão, but that was not the purpose of the visit. Years later, when I met Salomão as a refugee in Zaire, he told me how his treatment had changed, beginning from the day of my visit, until he was eventually released. He suspects that apart from the visit and the officials' awareness that he was known internationally, he might well have just disappeared like many others from the prisons.

When we were evacuated from Calambata in March of 1961 we little imagined that residence in Angola was finished for Virginia and the children. After four additional months at São Salvador, during which time many of the above events took place, I flew out to Luanda, then back to join my family in Boston in time for the birth of John Gordon.

Fourteen years intervened before I would set foot in Angola again. During this time my only contacts with Angolans would be made in the Congo. In September 1970 I began my service as general secretary of CBM. It was officially the Canadian Baptist Overseas Mission Board at that time, commonly referred to as CBOMB. In that capacity, and later as associate secretary, I made several visits to Angola.

For one of those visits, in 1975, I joined CBM colleagues Bob Malcolm and Eric MacKenzie at Kinshasa. From there we flew on to Angola,

In 1975, just before Angola's independence, the country had four rival armies, four flags. Represented here (L to R) Portuguese, FNLA, MPLA, Portuguese.

landing in Luanda. Hostilities had never ceased since 1961. It was a highly unstable period of transition from colonial to national rule. The country had spent these fourteen years in ceaseless conflict among three major conflicting parties—MPLA, FNLA and UNITA—occupied with fighting each other and the Portuguese colonial government's armed forces. The country was operating temporarily under four flags, four armies. It was a strange environment.

During that 1975 tour there was mini-bloodshed of a different sort. I had an encounter with bedbugs. We sent word ahead to Quimpondo telling of our arrival plans. Because I happened to be general secretary of CBM at that time, our hosts made a special effort on my behalf. Someone knew somebody who owned a mattress; I suspect its owner may have been a prostitute. A messenger was sent to commandeer the mattress for the special Canadian guest. My fortunate colleagues Bob and Eric were each given a sack of fresh hay or straw to sleep on. In the early

Bob and Margery Malcolm have been CBM's strongest ministry
link with Angola for more than four decades.

evening a number of the younger people stood around watching as the
mattress and the bags of straw were installed in the room where we were
to sleep. The old mission house had been opened for the occasion.

As soon as I lay down on that mattress I knew I was in deep trouble.
Bedbugs were boarding me like vultures thronging a carcass under the
African sun. I would get no sleep at all. Chuckles and joshing from Bob
and Eric.

"It must be nice to be a general secretary."

"Don't you feel sorry for us, having to sleep on straw?"

"Remember, we'll only be here for a week or so."

I got up in the darkness, put my pyjamas in a plastic bag and tied it in
a knot; they would be boiled at the next stop. Dusting my body off carefully, I dressed fully and sat in a wooden armchair for the remainder of
the night—and the remainder of my nights during that stay. It was impor-

tant not to offend those who had made special arrangements, so I would never reveal that I was not sleeping on the mattress.

We moved on as a trio to Cabinda. One day we found ourselves in a tight spot. We had gone to a cafe for refreshments. As we went in we noted that there were a half dozen soldiers there, in FNLA uniforms and with the predictable assault rifles beside them. Our Coca Cola and Fanta had just been served when the door opened and a dozen men walked in, also with assault rifles, but wearing different uniforms. This was the first appearance of MPLA troops in Cabinda. Theoretically the two forces, which had previously been rivals, were now to merge into one integrated army. The new contingent took their position on one side of us, the established group on the other, each sizing up the other very carefully. We were sitting in the highly uncomfortable middle. We guzzled our Cokes, paid the bill, and were out of there in record time.

In 1978 I also paid a serious visit to Angola, travelling alone. There was a strong presence of Cuban troops throughout the country, having come at the invitation of the MPLA faction. With Cuban help the MPLA forces were successful in subduing the north of the country and establishing a Communist government, although Jonas Savimbi and his UNITA movement were never vanquished, and still survive almost a quarter of a century later.

Because my visit to Angola did not relate in any way to the regime, and because I therefore lacked any official government document of approval apart from my visa, I did not have access to Angola's hotels. I went from one to another, and they failed to give me a room. There was no official refusal, no reason given. It is just that I always met the same replies. "Sorry, we're full." "Sorry, we have no place for you." That reaction seemed ridiculous in the light of the blatant evidence. The lobbies were empty, the hotels doing a good impression of a ghost town. Behind the registration desk stood banks of pigeon-holes, each with its key hanging in stark evidence of no trade, no sign of notes or letters in the boxes.

At one hotel, where absolutely nobody was in evidence other than the hotel clerk and me, he rolled his eyes upward and held his palms out and upward, in a signal that said graphically, "What can I do?" even though

When the CBM mission vehicle hit a land mine, lives were lost.

no word was spoken. He looked from side to side as a signal that he might be under observation. His "Sorry" seemed genuine. I began to realize that all the public hotels would give me the same answer, whatever their occupancy.

Taking a different approach, an Angolan pastor and I began walking the streets looking for a solution; it would have to be neither public nor private. To stay in a private home without government approval could bring danger to the family that received me. The population was still feeling its way into what was considered legal, what illegal. We found our solution in a small institution that would once have been a cheap hotel, but was currently being used as a lodging for war amputees. Some were in various stages of recovery, some simply incapacitated and no longer able to serve in the armed forces. An institution of this nature would not be under tight government surveillance, and they gave me a room for a couple of nights until I could get my flight to Cabinda.

This was perhaps the most depressing lodging I have ever used, because of the high percentage of children among those missing arms and legs. My sense of depression was heightened by my awareness that these children were combatants. I had already seen many in uniform who had not reached puberty. How proud they were to be carrying automatic weapons. I remember one lad in particular who hung around the entrance to this institution wearing a well-made uniform, one that might even have been tailored just for him. I judged that he might be ten or eleven. The empty left sleeve of his jacket was pinned up, and he wore a revolver proudly on his right hip. I don't doubt for a moment that it was loaded. His swagger seemed to be greatly admired by other children his age who thronged around him, most not in uniform, but missing limbs or extremities.

After we got a snack somewhere my friend went to stay with his relatives and I returned to my little room with its window facing the street. It was evening, and I had barely settled in when gunfire began, loud and very near. I put out my light and decided to sit it out on a chair in a corner, away from any line of direct fire. There were a few explosions, but mostly it was the rattle of automatic arms. I soon noted that this went on and on with something of a monotony that led me to wonder whether it was real. I got up and peered cautiously out the window, then immediately felt very foolish. There was an empty lot across the street. On the wall of a building a war movie was being projected at top volume. Government-sponsored public education and motivation were underway. The sound track was certainly realistic. I settled down for a solid night's sleep.

Arriving at Cabinda, where our family had served earlier, I received a tumultuous welcome. That night the people called a special meeting in the church, and it was very well attended. In Cabinda the church had more than just survived. In spite of turmoil, and despite the emergence of Communism, the churches in and around Cabinda had actually thrived. It was so strong that the Communist authorities had been able to neither suppress nor control it. The youth work was a prime example. In defiance of official policy, which forbade Christian youth activities, teams of young people continued to undertake evangelistic visits to villages and the countryside away from the city of Cabinda itself. In this district the church was still in an expansion mode and was riding the crest.

On our way to that night's meeting I noticed a jeep, with two Cuban officers, parked near the church building. They would observe; with the doors and windows wide open they would have no difficulty listening in on the activities, aided by the public address system. I'll admit that at that phase of my life, my first serious interaction with Communism, their presence made me nervous. My colleagues from Cabinda simply ignored their presence. When I had preached and the service had ended we all moved outside for social interaction around a campfire, where drumming, singing and joyous dancing were the order of the day. It may have been something like an hour later that I began first to hint, then to ask outright for permission to retire. The master of ceremonies declined. When I became more persistent he explained.

"This is not just for you, it's also for them to see." He pointed with his chin toward the observers in the jeep. "We're not allowed to protest against them, but we're permitted to demonstrate in favour of your visit. They see and they understand that you are loved and they are not. None of our people ever speak to them voluntarily or acknowledge their presence."

Experiences from later years when we served in Eastern Europe have cast a different light on the presence of those two Cuban officers in the jeep. Is it possible that one, or even both, of these officers were evangelicals from Cuba? They may even have been Baptists, for Cuban Baptists are certainly forced to serve in the army. This is pure speculation, but they may have hungered to hear both the music and the messages. If this were the case they would not have dared to reveal their identity and their faith.

When I was about to return by air to Luanda, I was waiting in the Cabinda airport with André Conga da Costa, general secretary of the *Igreja Evangélica De Angola*. I stood watching the incoming flight as it arrived from Luanda and began disgorging its passengers. They all seemed to be in uniform, carrying their automatic arms as they disembarked from this commercial flight. André stepped up to me quickly, his back to the window, requesting that I come away.

"Last week someone was arrested here for counting the troops arriving."

"Is it illegal to count civilians?" I asked.

"No."

"There were two." The plane was full, its capacity around 120 if I remember correctly.

André and I boarded the flight, and the plane filled with troops. In whichever direction I looked it seemed that somebody's machine gun was pointing at me. Some were stuffed in the racks overhead, others pushed under the seats. Some were lying across the laps of the travelling soldiers in whatever informal arrangement each one chose. I asked the soldier next to me if it wasn't a dangerous practice to actually bring the arms on board, rather than carrying them in the hold of the plane.

"No," he replied, pulling the long clip of bullets from a leg pocket of his army fatigues, "We don't travel with our guns loaded."

During this visit I became aware of a severe shortage of food in the city, the direct result of government policy. Unrealistic price controls kept the price of food below the cost of production. No gardener would deliberately work to raise and harvest food for the current prices, which were officially established. The second component, which worked hand in hand with the first, was that food could be sold legally only to official government buyers. If a farmer or gardener sold directly to a consumer (even to a friend), there were penalties. The seller was punished as a criminal, and likewise the buyer. As a result, gardens were planted only in remote areas where they would not be discovered, and the produce was sold "unofficially" to those willing to pay a market value.

A pastor pointed out how unwise legislation forced the entire population to be lawbreakers in order to survive. This resulted in a cheapening of all rules, regulations and laws, a direct contribution to lawlessness. Seeing the approach of an inspector, both buyer and seller were likely to run, and might well be shot in the process of running. To buy or sell on the black market was a crime. The entire population became involved full time in the process of either producing for the black market or of buying from it in order to survive. A government whose policies force close to one hundred percent of the population into criminal activity is conducting a flawed system. This greatly reduces any moral sense of right and wrong, and is essentially evil.

Most of the population was ready to talk in private about the flaws of a centralized planning system as practised in Angola, and even to laugh at it. Unless some of the details are shared, friends in Canada and elsewhere will fail to understand the complexity of the problems of sheer survival faced by our friends, brothers and sisters in Angola. Angolans are adamant that this story be told.

One of these discussions came up because a ship loaded with Bulgarian plums, preserved in metal-topped glass jars, had just unloaded at Cabinda port. The result was evident all around. Men, women and children were feasting on Bulgarian plums. Some were sitting at the curbs, drinking the juice and inhaling the plums, then spitting out the seeds. Some of this consumption took place while walking, standing in conversation, sitting in vehicles, everywhere, it seemed. Potatoes, rice, sardines, cooking oil, fresh fruit, cassava and much more might all be in critically short supply, but Bulgarian plums were available everywhere that day.

The same problems of availability and distribution were true, I was told, for hardware, consumer goods, textiles, appliances or whatever. No ship seemed to bring a mixed and balanced manifesto of goods. Where there was a lineup at an outlet, one's first reaction would be to run to secure a place in the queue, then to ask what was available for purchase. It might be hammers. Although a new hammer was not necessarily needed just now, one tended to buy it in order to trade it later for the saw or whatever else had become available to someone else who was in the right spot at the right time. But of course the act of privately selling a hammer would become an outlawed black market activity, punishable by fine, imprisonment or worse.

Functioning under these conditions, the church leadership decided to throw something of a banquet in honour of my visit. My hosts slaughtered a goat, prepared an abundance of vegetables, laid out a profusion of fruit on the tables, and brought soft drinks into the room in case lots.

Angolans João and Nora Matwawana, and Pedro Manuel were all present for dedication of new CBM headquarters in Mississauga. The Matwawanas have become Canadian citizens.

My protests at what I considered to be such waste were met with smiles, and with an insistence that people lived for occasions such as this.

"We enjoy it too, you know."

Stories around the table contrasted this scene with what was happening at an official level. Just that week the governor of the District of Cabinda had come in person to the church compound, appealing for assistance.

"You must help me save my honour. I have a visitor coming from a republic to the north of Cabinda. I need a goat."

No meat was available under the system he and his government had created. The population was careful to hide animals away, just as people maintained secret gardens, safely hidden away from confiscation. It was well known that within the wide sphere of influence of the Protestant churches a goat could always be found somewhere, as it was on this occasion. These exchanges became part of the mechanisms which, under restrictive regimes, became devices for survival.

A health problem emerged on that visit. I was showing the early symptoms of what was diagnosed weeks later as hepatitis. I had picked up the contamination on a visit to North Eastern Province of Kenya, short weeks before. On a particularly hot day in the desert I had given in to the purchase of an appealing orange squash, apparently mixed with unboiled water from the contaminated wells of Wajir. A nurse at Cabinda diagnosed my fever as being related to malaria, and gave me an injection to counteract that. The injection may have masked the emergence of the hepatitis symptoms.

When I got back to Canada I faced a publication deadline for the completion of my contribution to a composite book. The fatigue associated with hepatitis was making itself felt, enhanced by jet lag. After a day or so with my family I concluded that the best solution would be to isolate myself in a motel, working a few hours then resting a few hours, around the clock, until the writing was finished. That's the way I got it done, but it meant that I was out from under the observation of others. As I was shaving one morning I noticed the yellow cast of my eyes, my first clue that the fatigue was related to hepatitis. The chapter was finished, whether or not it was up to par.

My fatigue from hepatitis was so intense that CBM gave me the month of June 1978 to recuperate. Kenya, Angola and Canada are all intertwined in my memories of that bout with hepatitis. Yet in this, as in so many other unpleasant situations, I am able to look back and to see the amazing grace of God at work. That month apart was a time of physical and spiritual refreshment, both of which would prepare me for the events of July, when our son's serious accident would demand all our resources.

4
The Democratic Republic of Congo
As refugees to refugees

The Keith family's move to the Congo was in response to a surprise invitation that came after more than half a year of wondering what had happened to our career and what might be next. That was in 1961 and 1962, following our withdrawal from the hostilities in Angola. We had set out for Angola in 1957 with a clear sense of God's direction and purpose in our lives. Our wedding bands carried the inscription from a favourite Psalm, reinforcing a shared call to be part of the world mission of the church. My own inscription is still legible: "V.E.G to J.F.K. 6-11-55 PS. 2:8" That Scripture reads (NIV): *Ask of me, and I will make the nations your inheritance, the ends of the earth your possession.*

We had assumed that the geographical area to which God initially called us would be our permanent place of assignment, in a series of four-year episodes, for the rest of our lives. Wrong. Our departure from Angola in 1961 coincided with the start of a phase of world history that would be marked by continual rapid changes on the political landscape. That year in effect marked a watershed in the history of Canadian Baptist Ministries, as perhaps in other organizations. Since then it has no longer been practical to look to any specific country or assignment as being permanent. We were not yet aware of it in theory, but in practice, flexibility as to geographic assignment had already become an absolute requirement.

Looking back more than four decades later, I recall a sense of being ill at ease during those months in limbo. The uncertainty continued as we studied the 1962 letter of invitation drafted by Rev. David Grenfell.

David and his wife Margaret, with support from their Baptist Missionary Society of the U.K., had followed Angolan refugees into the Democratic Republic of the Congo. That country, the former Belgian Congo, was itself in a considerable measure of turmoil. David and Margaret had worked at a post called Quibocolo, near Angola's Maquela do Zombo. David and Juel Nordby, of the Methodist Mission, had gone to the Congo in 1961 and were mounting assistance programs for the several hundred thousand refugees who had crossed northward through the forests and plains from Angola into Congo.

David and Margaret had observed that hundreds of Angolans who had finished primary school in Angola would be able to take advantage of secondary school studies if any school would receive them. No existing school had the capacity to receive them, or the willingness to venture into such a program. David had secured permission from American Baptists to open a new school at Sona Bata, west of Kinshasa. Would we agree to head up the school, teach classes and direct it? Rumour had it that we spoke French. To the best of David's knowledge we were the only people available who spoke both French and Portuguese. French was essential, being the language of instruction; Portuguese was essential to hold the Angolan component together, especially at the beginning, for many of the Angolan students spoke little or no French. They would have to learn. I also had much French to learn.

Virginia already had her master's degree in romance languages and was a French teacher by profession; she was teaching French at Gordon College when we met. To affirm that John Keith spoke French at that time lies somewhere in the vague territory bounded by myths, wishes, exaggerations and outright prevarications. The reality was that we were ready and eager to be back in Africa, among many of the same people we had recently known there. Perhaps that is why we did not focus on my

The Keith residence at Sona Bata, Congo.

obvious linguistic deficiency, but agreed that with God's help we would give it a go.

We marvel at how, once again, the remarkable grace of God was at work. He took all of our deficiencies, combined with innocence, faith and outright audacity, and made the secondary school at Sona Bata into a remarkable institution that skyrocketed to some sort of local fame in a short, four-year period. A lot of credit is due in a number of directions, especially to the American Baptists at Sona Bata and Kinshasa, and their school inspector Lulendo. These people laid aside formalities and red tape. With utter selflessness, colleagues and officials struggled with us to open every door and overcome every obstacle. The school inspector closed his eyes to any upper age limit in the students we were admitting. I was heavy in my insistence that students over twenty-five years of age should be close-shaven to avoid drawing attention to first-year secondary students with beards.

These Angolan students were the most highly motivated set of youth I have ever met. They built and maintained a notable *esprit de corps*. They went beyond self-discipline to disciplining one another, both academically and in terms of conduct. Their performance also served as a stimulus to the Congolese who composed two-thirds of the student body, some excellent students among them. Within four years the Sona Bata students had lifted the school's results in the government-sponsored final exams to the top of the ranking.

Political tension was never more than a whisper away during those years. These were the years that logged the Stanleyville rebellion, the era of the infamous Simbas, the Mulele rebellion, the struggles around Patrice Lumumba, Antoine Gizenga and others. Battle lines seemed to be constantly shifting. Government, embassies and mission agencies all insisted that we who were serving in Congo in those days must have an evacuation plan ready. Rather than one plan, it was usually a question of choosing plan A, B or C, depending on the point of the compass from which the most recent threats and rumours seemed to have the greatest credibility. Confusion was rife, rumours abounded, and little could be affirmed with absolute certainty. There was a period when clean laundry did not go back into the dresser drawer, but into a ready-packed suitcase. In those days my first, treasured Gladstone bag, a gift from Mother and Dad, was still operational—the kind with a centre divider. Written on the divider was the same check-list of essentials I had used during the months of hostilities in Angola, to be ready to move at a moment's notice. It was valuable to have the pressing responsibilities of school to keep us focused.

As if worrying about the Republic's enemies was not enough, we had to consider how to protect ourselves from those who called themselves our friends. It seems that throughout the recent history of Congo there has always been one segment or another of the national army that was either on a rampage or on the loose in the countryside raising its own support. Being a soldier meant having a uniform and a gun; it did not necessarily involve either discipline or salary.

One of the constant preoccupations of the soldiers seems to have been their image. *"Faut respecter"* ("It is necessary to respect us") was often on their lips. Unfortunately the army produced remarkably little that would earn them that respect. Lynn Stairs, director of a technical training school for refugees, and I were on a tour of refugee villages on the day when General Joseph Mobutu (later Mobutu Sese Seko) seized power and proclaimed himself president. Travelling down a steep segment of the highway leading into the seaport of Matadi, we were flagged down most emphatically by a soldier carrying an automatic weapon.

"Now we're in power. You must respect us." We saluted and affirmed, "We respect."

This word respect carries a number of different meanings. We used it in the sense that the soldier demanded, and we complied with the outward manifestations he was looking for. Nothing more was required.

"Pass."

Military and police roadblocks were the bane of our existence, for there were endless reasons why we could not remain at our home base all the time. Financial transfers for the school and its building programs had to be cashed, local currency secured to pay workmen and teachers, supplies purchased for office, classroom, shop and home; and there was personal shopping to be done for the family as well as for the mission hospital just across the valley.

Between Sona Bata and Kinshasa there were two predictable, constant roadblocks. But there were often five and on occasion the number stretched to eight. To make this trip, which should take an hour and a half, one must then count on three or more hours, with endless haggling. An enterprising soldier or two required only their uniforms, weapons, two oil drums and a pipe or tree-trunk to mount a rather credible roadblock. In fact, the automatic weapons made a private road block look very credible indeed. And after all, once a road block had been set up, why bother to determine whether it was official or unofficial, for the results were the same.

The typical roadblock conversation had several components: (1) Identification – full documents required.(2) Point of origin and destination. (3) Accusation—"Aha! You have something in the back." Although said with a certain amount of glee (I've caught you), there was also the black tone of deep and unforgivable crime.

"Yes, we have some books for the school."

"No beer? No cigarettes?"

They soon learned that we tended not to be productive in beer or cigarettes, but we might well have something interesting to read, and they often settled for the healthiest reading material on the road. In the end, we were often waved through with a smile or a jovial comment, but the encounter never seemed to start that way. Those trips to Kinshasa (or anywhere else) were real food for ulcers for anyone so inclined. (4) Oh yes, the last component would be the invariable request for one of the soldiers or a camp follower to be given a ride and dropped somewhere along the way.

Soldiers without salary can become rather innovative. A sure contestant for one of the awards for best roadblock rationale was reported by student Joel after a weekend trip to Kinshasa. "Normal" transportation was on the back of a truck with a dozen or more other passengers, all piled on top of whatever full load the trucker was already carrying. The fares from his passengers were pure gravy for the driver. Joel reported on what he was sure was an impromptu roadblock; in fact we never heard of the incident again.

"Everybody down." The head soldier made an officious announcement that some watches had recently been stolen somewhere. He and his righteous team were hot on the trail of the thieves, and would make sure justice was done. To prove his or her innocence, each passenger with a watch had to produce the bill of sale for that watch, otherwise it would be assumed to be stolen property. When it came Joel's turn he argued a bit.

"Do you mean to say I have to give up this lousy watch that is eight years old just because I don't have the original receipt, long ago discarded?"

"Absolutely, look here. . ." The soldier showed half a bucket of watches he had collected. In those countries in transition from colonial rule to democracy, much of the population had no firm guidelines on what to expect from those in power. That is partly because under colonial rule there were passbook laws, travel control and many other restrictions that were neither logical to the people nor ever explained.

The reception for Prime Minister Moise Tshombe at Sona Bata was a gala affair.

There was one well-established and official roadblock situated on the crest of the hill at Binza, just west of Kinshasa. One sometimes arrived to find the barrier raised, in which case it was all right to drive right through. At least, that was the case in theory. One afternoon I had finished errands in Kinshasa and was hurrying past that raised barrier in hopes of reaching Sona Bata before nightfall. In my eagerness I made an error in judgement that could have proved fatal.

Just as I reached the barrier a soldier ran out from the shelter set up a few metres back from the highway. He tried to flag me down, using the more casual symbol that indicated a request for a ride rather than the raised hand or blown whistle that normally signalled an official "halt." My quick judgement call was to ignore his signal and drive right through. I glanced in my rear view mirror. He had run to the middle of the road behind me, drawn his pistol and was bringing it down for a shot. I locked my brakes, dragging the tires, then reversed to where he now stood by the side of the road. I took the initiative before he could speak, and chose not to reveal that I knew he had drawn his pistol.

"Good afternoon. Is there something I can do for you?" His response was now equally open and friendly.

"Why yes. Could you give me a ride to the hospital at Sona Bata?"

Of course I would. He got in beside me and exchanged pleasantries all the way. He was going to visit his girl friend at the hospital. He knew, of course, that if I had not stopped he would have fired at me. What he didn't know, (and I chose not to tell him), is that I knew this as well.

It was never a joy to be on those roads at night. There were potholes. Dark-skinned people in dark clothes and carrying no light could be expected to be using the road either on foot or on bicycle. They were often extremely hard to see. Breakdowns were frequent and the vehicles might remain right there on the road until parts were secured. The local convention was to go back a few metres and throw brush on the road to signal "accident ahead." Some of the perils were reduced as one gained experience and learned to read the signs. At the end of a safe trip undertaken at night one was always conscious of the grace of God.

For those in positions of authority, distinctions between what was official and what was private were shady at best. Shortly after our arrival I required a driver's permit, and wondered how complicated the process might prove to be, recalling the weeks on end it took in Portugal. It turned out to be not too difficult after all—for those who had francs to spend. The blank forms under the counter had a number of boxes that could be stamped with a round and very official rubber stamp, each stamp giving permission to drive a different conveyance. The stamp was soon poised in the air, and any driver testing process waived with a smile. Did I drive a car? Whack. A heavy truck? Whack. A motorcycle? Whack. A bus? Whack. Enough . . . no, I don't drive a train or other conveyance. Oh yes, three photos. We had travelled to Congo well equipped with a profusion of passport-size photos, just for occasions like this. But three of them? Standard procedure called for only two photos, and my mind clicked on the question but I didn't ask it—my day was going too well so far.

The man at the wicket asked whether my wife would also like a driver's licence. Yes she would, and I secured it for her on the spot. The man seemed disappointed that Virginia drives neither bus, motorcycle nor heavy truck. Without asking, I forked over three photos of Virginia as well. More than a year passed before the riddle of three photos was solved. I was in a post office somewhere when approached by a well dressed and very pleasant person who began a conversation. I eventually asked where we had met before.

"Oh, don't you remember me? I'm the one who issued your driver's licence. See, I have your photo right here in my wallet." I didn't ask what he did with Virginia's

Thomas Nlandu, with wife and daughters by their house at Sona Bata, succeeded John Keith as high school director.

photo and I won't speculate. With my photo he certainly would do a bit of name-dropping about his good friend the director of the secondary school at Sona Bata.

Life at Sona Bata was too hectic to permit any regular hunting expeditions, but it was important to get to know my workmen from the carpenter shop. Many a time there would be a few minutes to perch up on a work bench and listen to their hunting stories. Mota and Norbert used hunting dogs and had their own homemade firearms. One day Mota had a serious swelling of his right eye and a bad burn on the same cheek. Most hunters turned their heads away at the last minute to avoid powder burns, which may account in part for a low level of marksmanship. Mota had not done that, and he paid the price, but it was not serious enough to lose his eyesight.

The hunting dogs were each fitted with a wooden, carved bell. Attached to a vine, it was tied around the dog's middle just ahead of the back legs. These hunting bells had a distinctive rattle faintly reminiscent of a camel's bell, which is also from carved wood. I felt sorry for the dogs because they were virtually starved just before hunting days, to give their appetites a keen edge. Where big game was involved hunting dogs would be called in to track and locate wounded animals. Mota and Norbert used their dogs to flush or tree small game, as the Sona Bata region had already at this time been stripped of most significant game animals. These men readily shared how and where the local armourer worked, which was of significant interest. His rule was that the client must produce the gun barrel and a piece of appropriate valuable wood for the stock. The task of the gunsmith was to manufacture trigger, hammer, side plates, springs and other parts from local metal. Truck springs were favoured as a source of steel for this remaining hardware.

On a visit to Sona Bata several years after our assignment there had ended we were greeted cordially and enthusiastically by a wide range of people, but the lasting memories are of Norbert's greeting. He was a short man, thinly built but well muscled. When he saw me coming he stretched his arms wide and, with a long whoop, came running straight at me. I was quite unprepared for his flying leap, which ended in something like a bear hug, his legs somewhere around my hips. Our workmen had not become church members, but when it came my turn to preach from time to time, they were usually in attendance.

Having been so afraid of pain in my younger years, I admired the tolerance for pain shown by Congolese and Angolans both. Late one evening a runner arrived with news that there had been a serious accident. Would it be possible to take the pickup truck to bring some of the injured to our Sona Bata mission hospital? The accident was within five or ten minutes by road. A truck fully loaded with cases of beer empties had gone off the road at a curve in the highway, and had struck a tree. The load of passengers riding on top had been scattered through the forest, and were bleeding from a variety of injuries.

At the hospital a bevy of male and female nurses trained and accustomed to such tasks were soon gowned and at work on what was very

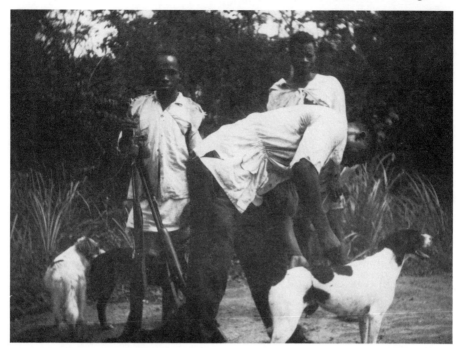

A hunting trip with men from the carpentry shop at Sona Bata.

much like a quilting bee. Staying on to visit with the patients, I noted that hospital director Makengo had arranged them in what appeared to be his order of priority according to loss of blood. The two bleeding most profusely were toward the beginning of the line, which had probably a dozen people in all, lined up on benches. One required extensive stitching across the leg above the knee. A second patient appeared to have been scalped by a branch, the flap was being sewn back into position. All this without a word of complaint or wailing from any of them. That became even more admirable when those plying the needles ran out of local anaesthesia. There were still no complaints, no moaning.

At the end of the line sat a man with no evident wounds—the reason he was placed at the end. When his turn came he walked into the operating room with no external evidence that he required attention. When asked what his problem was he still said not a word. He couldn't. Pointing to his mouth, he revealed his tongue hanging at an odd angle. "Up you go," they said, putting him on the operating table and proceeding to stitch his tongue back into position.

As he lay on the operating table he, like those before him, would have read the inscription on the ceiling above him. Written in Kikongo, the inscription was straightforward: *"Beto tugubilanga, Kansi Nzambi oyalanga."* Many had found help on that same table reading the same inscription: "We operate, but it is God who cures."

Dr. Glen Tuttle, who founded that hospital and another large hospital at Kimpese, is perhaps the most remarkable medical person I have known on any continent. He considered himself a missionary first and a doctor/ surgeon only incidentally. Having said that, he was an outstanding doctor, surgeon and administrator. Dr. Tuttle was among the best at making the transition from the old regime of colonial days to the new era of africanization in medicine as in other administrative matters. He travelled the villages at the outset of his career, choosing young men in bare feet whom he sponsored and trained through various phases to the point that they were regularly doing caesarean sections, hernia surgery and other limited procedures. They became, at first, his full colleagues. Then by his deliberate choice, in the years while we were living together there at Sona Bata, they became his directors and Glen was happy to stay on and work under them. Not everyone whose career had begun in the colonial era made such an easy transition through the era when nationalism came to the fore. Dr. Tuttle served as a true model for that transitional process. He lived in the shadow of the life of Jesus, who came not to be served but to serve others and to give his life so that others might live.

From time to time, my handy bicycle permitted a quick visit to the hospital, perhaps after classes had finished for the day. One day an army jeep had come in, and I arrived to see three soldiers literally stuffing a fourth person, obviously a patient, into a pair of army coveralls. It is not easy to get into coveralls under the best of conditions. This soldier's limbs were being bent in directions they didn't seem to want to go. His soldier colleagues were not being gentle, and the man seemed to be complaining a bit. In view of the generally high threshold of pain that I had observed, I enquired what was up. Yes, the patient was a soldier, and it seems that they had been sent to take him back to the army base, and he

The student body, 1964, in front of Sona Bata High School.

shouldn't go in civvies. Asking what his problem was, I was told that a jeep had run over him lengthwise. He was obviously a survivor, in spite of his colleagues.

Dr. Tuttle was the personal physician to Zaire's first President, Joseph Kasa-Vubu. From time to time the presidential limousine would appear, passing by our house and school on its way to our hospital. Other notable guests included the president's personal secretary, who came occasionally for treatment or rest, and we became friends. Somewhat more unexpected, Prime Minister Moise Tshombe came to be a guest in our house twice in the same day. He and his entourage of a dozen or so came for a planned tea break just before the regional thanksgiving service at which he was the guest speaker. Refreshments were also going to be served after the service, but his attendants waited until the last minute to mention that there had been threats against his life, and that this special guest would not be allowed to eat in public. In fact, he needed to be fed in a private home, and right away at that, for his cavalcade would need to leave within the hour. Dr. Kimpiatu and I were immediately in the storehouse of our home, where we spared no measure in opening cans of whatever was available. It was a jovial occasion behind the scenes, the kind that firms up bonds of friendship and makes for lasting memories.

No members of our family were ever actually patients at the hospital, but from time to time we needed Dr. Tuttle's help and his advice. At one point all of five us were plagued by an itch. Dr. Tuttle diagnosed the problem immediately as scabies, and prescribed a troublesome set of measures that involved very careful attention to scrupulous cleanliness, with constant boiling of all sheets, towels and clothing. My case seemed to be the worst, and he prescribed some sort of tranquilizer to lower the irritation. The problem was that life had to go on.

The medication turned out to be more life threatening than I had perceived. A new and elaborate bell tower had been added to the church at Kasangulu. Having worked as a tree surgeon I was accustomed to heights, and volunteered to be part of the crew that would put the metal roof in place. It was a strange arrangement, the small assembled cone being lifted up through the middle of the tower with ropes. It was a slow, tedious process, and as a result of the medication I drowsed off while perched up there astride the wall. Fortunately I caught myself before I fell, but the memory of that bizarre incident remains as one of the closest calls of an entire career. And all because of the itch! Students had brought the itch to school. Contact with the desk of an infected student was enough to transfer it to my wrists and forearms. For Virginia, involved in a full teaching program while being mother and homemaker, the extra laundry that this boiling treatment required was a nightmare. Laundry itself was an elaborate process involving a washing machine powered by a small gas engine. It sounded something like running a lawn mower in the house—a lawnmower with a defective muffler.

It was a brash and highly illogical move to have accepted—without having appropriate proficiency in the French language—the directorship of a secondary school that must function in French. Furthermore, in my years of preparation I had never taken a single course in principles or procedures of education. Utter folly.

The situation was complicated by the very new and confusing state of post-independence education in Congo. The new republic's educational authorities had rejected the entire set of Belgian colonial text books, even those dealing with neutral subjects such as science and mathematics. A surprisingly elaborate curriculum had been issued, specifying in considerable detail the material to be taught—but without providing a single textbook. Each teacher and each school had to solve that problem on site. It required extensive preparation as well as the duplication of materials for some lessons and for all examinations on a spirit duplicator. The first year was most difficult. By the second year some text books were becoming available.

Obstacles in the academic and administrative spheres included teacher strikes (the government was often months behind in the payment of its teachers) and student strikes as well. There may have been problems and obstacles, but boredom was not one of them.

There was a remarkable and creative musical environment in our school, with two excellent choral groups of broadcast quality. A competition raged between them, each attempting to come up with a new production (both words and music) for each successive Sunday worship. The musical component of worship was never dull, and to curtail the time for music would have been disheartening after such effort. The surprising component lies in how much of this music survived. Years later, travelling in Angola I heard composition after composition sung in Kikongo, pieces that dated back to those years in Sona Bata, Congo. It was a creative time in church music.

The crowning event of these four years happened one memorable afternoon, quite unannounced. A trim young man of modest bearing in a dark suit walked up to the school, his tie loosened, his jacket carried over his arm.

"My name is Thomas Nlandu and I've come to help you," he said simply. I had repeatedly heard that three young men related to this school system were studying in the United States for their master's degrees in education. They would return to teach and direct schools in this particular part of the school system, which related to what is now the Baptist Community of Western Congo. I had no hope that our school would be

Sona Bata High School had several choral groups that composed words and music.

in line to receive one of them. In my opinion we got the very best, and he made a difference immediately.

During our last year in Congo, Nlandu worked as my associate, then assumed excellent leadership of the school until he was drafted to become legal representative for the entire network of churches. Today he is the Bible Society's secretary for Congo. My deepest regret in that relationship is that I did not leave him a better heritage in furnishings and equipment. Nlandu is a most extraordinary man in terms of dedication, ability, training and humility.

That first set of students who went through Sona Bata went on to make a remarkable impact on both Angola and Congo. They proceeded on scholarships to schools and universities all over the world. Two, at least, became medical doctors; others participated in government. By the grace of God, and in spite of assorted deficiencies and defects, the adventure that was Congo was not, in the end, a disaster.

Half a continent away and a decade later, as general secretary of CBM in the 1970s, I participated in opening up new contacts for CBM in Kivu province of eastern Congo, the region bordering on Rwanda and Burundi. Still later, when the ethnic conflicts of the 1990s developed around Goma it was already familiar territory, an area in which CBM personnel were already serving.

In the 1980s, at which time I was associate secretary, Virginia accompanied me on a visit to Kivu, along with Malcolm Card. Virginia and I were very conscious of the calendar, for January 18, 1986 was the first anniversary of the fire that had destroyed our home in Ontario. By the grace of God we had awakened at about 3:15 a.m. to find the house in

Travel in Congo was often an adventure. This road was in Kivu province.

flames, and had escaped with our lives. Considering the seven hours of adjustment for time zones, we should be in the air at the moment of anniversary, flying with Mission Aviation Fellowship pilot Andy Briggs. Our flight would be out of Goma to Nebobongo, then on to a different project near Bondo in north central Congo.

Our takeoff that morning was normal. Our flight path would take us between the twin volcano peaks of Nyiragongo and Nyamuragira, just north of Goma. As the heaviest passenger, I sat in the co-pilot's place next to Andy. Malcolm and Virginia were in the seats behind us. We had reminded each other that we would take note of that anniversary moment at 10:15, remembering our deliverance the year before. We noted, and will probably never forget. At that time we were precisely between the two volcano peaks when suddenly fog closed us in. Andy was unable to spot the precise location of the peaks. He told us we would not be safe until we got above 3,500 metres, permitting us to clear the highest of the

Bob Malcolm with colleagues. CBM work in Eastern Zaire straddled the equator.

two. He put the plane into a tight circle and began clawing upward for elevation. The sun showed enough of a bright spot through the fog that I was able to tick off spirals as he made them. There were seven. At 11,500 feet by the altimeter we began to level off. Andy had pushed his plane to extremes that would later be questioned by MAF, extremes signalled by the periodic buzzing of the warning signal that our angle of climb was too steep for safety. We could not have been in better hands – the Lord's and those of MAF pilot Andy Briggs. We came through safely, another of those evidences of the grace of God.

We came to appreciate other MAF pilots as well, and were flying with two of them on the day when President Musevene of Uganda captured his capital city, Kampala, from the former regime of Idi Amin. We took off from a little airstrip in north Kivu and our destination that day was Nairobi, Kenya. The MAF pilots normally touched down at Kampala, a convenient place for refuelling, but they had not done so on their flight from Nairobi that morning. They reported that the battle for Kampala

Visiting with Angolan refugees in Congo, living along the Atlantic coast.

airport had been underway as they flew over it. With his droll sense of humour our pilot made a tongue-in-cheek comment to the effect that since he had enough fuel to get us within five kilometres of the Nairobi airstrip, he didn't plan to touch down at Kampala on our flight back either.

Our flight path to Nairobi that afternoon took us roughly over the Kampala airstrip, and our pilot drew attention to it. Through the miniature binoculars I carried the airport seemed peaceful below us. Our pilot also announced that the skyline of Kampala was visible on our left, due north. I had just trained my binoculars on the city when a huge fire-ball blossomed there. I made a mental note that it reached higher than the high rise buildings. Our flight to Nairobi's smaller Wilson airport was completed without incident. That night Kenya's television newscast announced the fall of Kampala to the Musevene forces, and mentioned that the ammunition dump had been blown up. Yes indeed it had, and we knew precisely when.

None of my own experiences in Kivu would even begin to approach the dramatic nature of deliverances experienced by CBM colleagues who lived and worked there. The names Loden and Foster come immediately to mind, along with Connie Smith, Hope Slessor, the Waldocks and the Matwawanas (the same João Matwawana who had been our student in Calambata later served with both the BMS and CBM in refugee work in Congo). My account is not an attempt to outdo the experiences of others, but only to relate what I have experienced first hand. It is also my hope that this account will help those who follow missionaries carefully in prayer to understand something of the range of experiences they are likely to face from time to time.

5
Canada
Tried as though by fire

In August of 1970 our household goods and personal possessions were moved by rental truck from Massachusetts to Burlington, Ontario, close enough to Toronto for daily commuting to my new position at CBM headquarters (still CBOMB at that time). Our twenty years based in Canada would include ten as general secretary, then another decade as associate secretary. The work involved extensive travel as I focused on researching and initiating new ventures overseas, working toward non-traditional models of relationships that would be appropriate to the post-colonial era. After my switch to associate secretary in 1981 Virginia travelled with me, often for six months at a stretch, as we explored new opportunities and assessed existing Canadian programs overseas. Both as general secretary and as associate secretary the periods spent outside Canada contained strong components of ministry to overseas churches as well as to missionaries.

Our Burlington home was on a quiet street in a peaceful neighbourhood that gave our children easy access on foot to the nearby schools they would attend. The perils of Angola and Congo were behind us. Surely this would be a safe and secure spot for our family.

On a sunny July morning in 1978 I picked up my office phone to take a call from the hospital in Hamilton. All my priorities were immediately reordered. The pressing urgency of reports, problems to be solved, communications, phone calls to be made, meetings to attend faded to nothing. A colleague drove me to the intensive care unit at Hamilton General Hospital. I knew little except that our sixteen-year-old son John was unconscious, seriously injured, and that he had fallen from a tree while rescuing a kitten.

The grace of God that eventually brought back John's consciousness, and weeks later his mobility, dates back to the night before the accident, when I had put the sprinkler out to water our lawn. The summer was a dry one, and that watering of the lawn appears to have given it just enough sponginess to make a difference. The crotch of the oak where John had retrieved the kitten was later pointed out by preschool children who had been watching. It was about fifteen metres, roughly forty-five feet, above the ground. Our daughter Carol, twenty-one at that time, was in the house and heard the thump; it was she who phoned for the ambulance.

Virginia was already at the intensive care unit when I arrived. Dr. Jim Murray's words offered no encouragement.

"Your son is in very serious condition."

I went in to stand beside his convulsive body, and could not hold back the words. "Johnny, this is your Dad. I love you very much." I was immediately told, rather brusquely I thought, that John was unconscious and could not hear me. Somehow that was irrelevant to this pouring out of my deepest emotions. Never had I so fully understood, as at that moment, the significance of words I had known since childhood: *"For God so loved the world, that He gave His only begotten son, that whoever believes in Him should not perish, but have eternal life"* (John 3:16, NASB).

This was my only son, unconscious and partially paralyzed before me, and I knew how much I would be willing to give if only the trauma, the injury, the damage and the pain would all go away. How great was the deliberate sacrifice that God in Jesus expended on behalf of an errant and rebellious world.

There beside the emergency room table they talked to me first of the comparatively superficial injuries which could potentially heal. His pelvis was fractured and there were internal injuries caused by bone fragments. Before they mentioned his broken arm, I noticed that it was at an angle.

"Aren't you going to do something about it?" I asked.

"No, we're going to wait and see if he lives first." That reply, by one of the hospital personnel born on another continent, was not characteristic of the care, which, in general, we found to be very considerate. That doctor responded positively to my indignation, pulled the arm and realigned it temporarily, asking, "There, is that better?"

They also spoke of the more serious obstacle, the brain-stem injury, which none of them expected to heal. They offered no glimmer of hope that John would again participate in a normal life. Survival itself was doubtful. If he were to survive one could expect that he would be "a vegetable," unable to communicate, unable to feed himself or care for his bodily needs.

The following days and nights have become a memory blur. Virginia and I spent the first night by his side, then visited daily for as long as I could stand it. Then I had to get away, leaving the visitation to other family members. In the next stages God worked his grace through a combination of superb hospital skills and care combined with the patient hour-by-hour recovery talk-a-thon that was Carol's significant contribution at her little brother's bedside. In long vigils day after day she spoke slowly and quietly in his ear.

"John, this is Carol. You've had an accident. . ."

"John, you're in the hospital. Your family is here. . ."

"John, if you can hear me, squeeze my hand. . ."

Hospital personnel asked if Carol had had special training in this kind of therapy. She had not. She was just doing all the right things instinctively.

Separated from John's bed by only a curtain was another young man in a Stryker frame, the victim of a car accident. Weeks later he told us how much Carol's work with John had meant for him personally, how it had helped him in keeping his own courage alive through the long, hard nights as she talked to John or read stories to him in his unconscious state. John carries no memory of the part that Carol played, but we believe it had a profound effect on his will to live and his determination to fight his way back to normal existence.

Various family members each had a different role to play: Virginia's steady faithfulness in daily visits, Mother's coming from New Brunswick to spend day after day with John as he regained consciousness and before he had regained his social graces, Shirley's active part in visiting and in physical rehabilitation once he regained his mobility. The grace of God is implemented through many avenues.

The events of my life and experience all fortify the credibility that a personal God—the God who has revealed himself in the Scriptures and in Jesus—interacts with us in the intimacy of our private lives. That the God of the macrocosm should be directly involved in the detail of our microcosm goes against all logic. It is part of the mystery and the marvel of who he is and how he relates to us. Our own deliberate and willing acceptance of the reality that he is in charge of the world around us, and in charge of our lives, is crucial to our relationship with him. This does not imply that God can be manipulated to bring about our wishes or desires. It does, however, permit us to arrive at a state of peace while we are still in trauma, for he is ultimately in charge.

Since that time, and for the encouragement of two people who felt that their lives were beyond hope, I have drawn together the experiences we went through as a family in the course of John's recovery. The following notes are copied directly from the notebook in which I carry prayer requests and other material of a very personal nature:

Peace and Wholeness

*To move toward the peace and wholeness which I desire and which God desires for my life, I must move through a series of **acceptance factors**, which are the given conditions of a walk with him:*

*1. That the **Lordship of Jesus** is basic. I am to move into a state of joyful acceptance of that lordship. Rebelliousness and peace are mutually exclusive conditions. To rule my own life is a luxury I am not granted.*

*2. That **God is at work** and he is working in my life. His purpose includes accomplishing things and conditions in me. My relationship to him is of higher value than achievement factors.*

*3. That **he uses some events and measures to accomplish his will that I would not choose,** but which I must learn to accept, even to welcome.*

*4. That I cannot normally expect to see the pattern of what God is doing while I am still in the midst of situations. **His pattern emerges in retrospect.***

*5. That he begins to move or alter conditions once **I accept, and cease to rebel against adverse situations** in which I find myself.*

> *But to the degree you share the sufferings of Christ, keep on rejoicing, so that also at the revelation of His glory you may rejoice with exultation.*

(1 Peter 4:13, NASB)

In John Gordon's long, and sometimes dramatic, road back to recovery he moved through a series of phases. Each phase was very difficult to accept at the time. Yet it seems that when we came to accept and be thankful for the measure of answered prayer that God had given us, then he moved us on to the next phase. It was this process that led me to draw together the above lists of "acceptance factors."

First, as John hung between life and death we prayed for his survival. Within days it was becoming evident that he would survive but that he would probably be a vegetable for the rest of his days, with the dramatic changes in lifestyle this would imply for all of us. God had answered our first prayer, in which we had been joined by a chain of many people, stretching all around the world, but in his own way, and with a distinct departure from what we had in mind. A son who could not walk, talk or even feed himself? When we had accepted that, and learned to be grateful for it, a new phase emerged.

Over the course of weeks, consciousness began to return, one small sign at a time. There was a flickering of the eyelids. Carol's bedside coaching led to a series of yes/no communications. First, there was just the squeeze of a hand, such a momentous thing at the time. This developed into clearer signs. Lifting one finger indicated "yes" to the question; two fingers signalled "no." Verbal communications were not possible because of the life support tubes that were fed into his body through John's tracheotomy, the scars of which are still visible in his neck today.

John's right side was still paralyzed, an additional obstacle to be overcome in a right-handed person. What an enormous breakthrough in communications came on the day he reached for pencil and a pad of paper with his left hand, and wrote a squiggly note complaining about the day's enema! We had been ardently praying to have our son back. Of course the prayer implied that we wanted him back whole, in every way. We were not professionally aware of all the variations that might be added in the answering of that prayer. When we had accepted that, and learned to be grateful for it, another phase emerged, albeit a short one, lasting no more than a few days.

This phase emerged when John's tracheotomy tubes had been removed and he was promoted to a wheelchair. He was now at Chedoke Hospital in a different part of Hamilton. A very definite and rather drastic personality change had come about, evidenced in both action and language. John blurted out phrases that left us wide-eyed. He showed a new rebelliousness of spirit, an assertion of identity, an insistence on going into parts of the hospital labelled as being out of bounds, all of which were out of character with the John we knew. I remember John's determined attempt, during one of our wheelchair strolls through the corridors at Chedoke, to lift himself from his wheelchair just to peer through the double windows of a set of swinging doors that had been chained shut. The prohibition was there and evident, so he had to see what was beyond it.

The healing brain, in its recovery process, was taking John through uncharted territory. Coming as a surprise, this was one of the very difficult phases to accept. Acceptance came. This was the new John we had been given. We were grateful, and we would adjust. But John himself was still in transition, and he lingered in that phase of altered personality for less than a week in all.

One of the very difficult lessons in life is to learn to pray with sincerity the prayer that Jesus prayed in the garden of Gethsemane on the night before he was crucified: *My Father, if it is possible, let this cup pass from me; yet not as I will but as Thou wilt* (Matthew 26:39 NASB).

It seems we had no sooner prayed this prayer with acceptance and thanksgiving for having this much of our son back, when God moved him on to a still more complete wholeness. The lesson we learned was not about how to manipulate God, but about how to live in peace with what God gives.

Hospital staff at Chedoke were cautious not to raise our expectations too high.

"We will probably keep him here two years. We'll do our best; we promise you nothing." The accident had occurred on July 17. Before the end of September we were called in for a conference.

"You can take John home in two weeks; all objectives have been accomplished." If there was ever a consciousness of the grace of God at work it was on that day. Our family doctor summarized well the amazement of the professionals.

"The healing of the body is a marvellous process. But as far as I'm concerned, what happened from here up was a miracle." He indicated the neck and head.

Colleagues at Canadian Baptist Ministries had set up phone links for special prayer, a web of communication that reached to God from what we tend to consider remote corners of our world. This was in the era before fax and e-mail communications. One Sunday morning we had just finished breakfast when a phone call from Kenya requested news on specific progress, to be shared with other colleagues there. No sooner had that call ended when a similar one came in from the Andes, as colleagues in Bolivia wanted to be brought up to date. It was with great meaning that we finished devotions around the table by singing, "I'm so glad I'm a part of the family of God."

Twenty years later, a married man in a family of five, John still works at sorting out what facets of his long-term career development have been

John with twin sons Andrew and Benjamin (1998).

influenced by frontal lobe damage that was not reported to us at the time of the accident. In the early months, while partial paralysis of his right side was still diminishing, he developed ambidextrous skills. John returned to his studies, completed high school, and went on to complete a bachelor's degree in physical education at McMaster University then an education degree at the University of Western Ontario. These days the profound joy of living only twenty minutes from John and Judy, the sheer enjoyment of sharing their twin boys and older daughter Alexandra, draw from us many glimpses back over the difficult road along which we experienced so much of the grace of God.

The burning boat episode, another demonstration of God's grace, took place in New Brunswick in July of 1982. During a CBM furlough conference in Moncton a special outing was arranged at a cottage on Main River, to include a lobster feast and an outing on the river in a wooden lobster boat that had been converted to a pleasure craft. The boat's capacity was about three dozen people, so two tours were scheduled.

Ours was the second outing. Virginia and I were on the front deck, sitting cross-legged in conversation with a colleague. We were interrupted from time to time by Robert Cowan, a ten-year-old boy who was enjoying the outing, as were a number of other children. God's acts of grace that day included an exploratory trip that Robert, small for his age, took into the front cabin under the deck where we were sitting. It had bunks and cushions, perhaps a life preserver or two, all very interesting to explore. Robert tapped on the skylight to get my attention. I motioned to the catch; he undid it from the inside, and I lifted back the hatch. It was just the right size for him to come up through, so I reached down and lifted him out, onto the deck beside us. The hatch remained unlocked, and Robert stayed with us on the front deck. All this became significant scant minutes later.

The boat stopped and the owner could not get it restarted. The propeller shaft bearing had overheated and seized. In our part of the boat conversation continued; these things sort themselves out. Before long a commotion from the back of the boat caught our attention. A wisp of smoke was curling up from the stern. On the rear deck passengers were hurriedly folding and stacking lawn chairs. In retrospect, this was the mistake of the day, for the piled chairs impeded access to the life preservers stored around the perimeter. It would have been easy to toss all the metal chairs overboard, but who could have known that we were to be faced with a real disaster rather than an inconvenience?

Some people were being loaded already into the small tender that was towed behind the boat. It became evident rather quickly that we should make provision for getting into the water. Looking down through that open hatch, which was too small to let me through, I could see cushions and a life jacket or two. I lowered Robert in there again, and he passed the items to me. These articles floated a number of people.

There were a number of courageous acts that day. Doris Smith, secretary in CBM's Saint John office, was already safely aboard the little tender when she heard someone still on board the boat say, "But I can't swim."

"Well, here, take my place," said Doris, and got back on the boat, which by now was in flames. Then Doris quietly commented, "I can't swim either." Doris was one of those who was given a life preserver, and she was eventually picked up safely.

We on the front deck could see no advantage to be gained by going to the stern. Even though the prow was higher than the stern, one by one people made their way into the water as flames began to lick along the back of the boat. My last personal observation as I cast my eye around the deck was to see a scattering of footwear. There, in the midst of this confusion, was a little pair of canvas deck shoes, the cheapest from Bata, neatly tied together. Virginia Keith is never one to walk away leaving anything in disorder.

Being a strong swimmer, Virginia made it to shore without a life preserver. She helped another woman to where she could get a firm grip on the edge of the little tender. The people in the tender were not used to rowing, so the two women hanging on to the outside, kicked to help propel it to shore.

Robert was still with us at the front. He was holding a child's life preserver he had rescued out of the forward cabin, but he was reluctant to go in the water. His parents (non-swimmers) and his toddler sister Shelly Anne were safely in the tender. I took Robert with me and slipped his life preserver over one of my shoulders, welcoming whatever buoyancy it could provide for the two of us, as I am by no means a good swimmer. He and I slipped as gently as possible over the port side and into the water.

I knew we were in trouble immediately as this lad, with his fear of the water, kept trying to climb higher and higher on me, and I was having trouble keeping my head high enough to breathe. I twisted him around so his arms were flailing outward, and whispered to him that Jesus would take care of us. The immediate calming effect that the name of Jesus had on this young boy was amazing, and it is a witness to the teaching his parents had given him in the home.

"Yes," he said eagerly, "Jesus will look after us." From that point there was no more panic, no thrashing around, indeed no more problem.

The thirty-five people on the boat that day had included children, infants, elderly folks, non-swimmers and people with heart conditions. By the grace of God there was not a single direct casualty. A man on shore, painting his house, saw what was happening and phoned the home of our host, where our other colleagues were gathered. Many families were divided between the boat's two outings. Residents from a nearby First Nations reservation were the first to pick up survivors.

I remember the relief of being given a proper life preserver, which made it possible to float until others had been picked up and they came back for me. The jubilation of the reunion and the service of thanksgiving the following morning, I am not able to describe. Reactions varied widely. For me, the stimulus and exhilaration of the event made it a three- or four-lobster day. For another, and I respect the attitude, the reaction was, "How can one think of eating when God has so evidently worked such a great deliverance!"

The most highly touching moment for me was when Robert slipped up to me and put a piece of "Bazooka" bubble gum in my hand. For three years that little treasure was stored in a silver plated cup inscribed *Jackie,* the cup I had used as a child, which sat on a shelf by my desk. When I list the treasures lost in our house fire a few years later, I include that mug and its precious treasure, my gift from the ten-year-old boy who was my fellow survivor.

In 1980, when proximity to the Toronto office was no longer as important for our work with CBM, we had moved to Clear Lake, Ontario. In the early morning of January 18, 1985 our house with all its contents, burned. We had been to Vancouver on assignment, and got home late from the airport. Virginia had done some washing and ironing in the evening, as we were to leave the next day for a CBM retreat. Just after three a.m. I awakened to the sound of the smoke alarm, the smell of smoke and the pop of something, perhaps an aerosol can. I woke Virginia, asked her to get her glasses and hearing aids and to start the car.

Looking at how the grace of God was mediated through circumstances, I would mention that our house had a deck, with direct access from the bedroom through a sliding door. Furthermore it was our habit to leave the car unlocked in the driveway, with a spare key hidden but easily accessible inside.

Virginia went out via the deck, wrapped in a blanket. When I looked through the bedroom door to the living room the house was a sheet of flame. Even so I was able to lift my winter jacket off the sofa by the door. I could not find my glasses. We drove down Birchview Road looking for a year-round resident who could let us in to phone the fire department;

then we went back to await the fire trucks at the intersection and direct them. Ron Slomka, from whom we purchased our house, lived across the lake. He had seen the fire and raced across the lake on his snowmobile. We would spend the rest of the night at his house. When inspectors examined the charred house remains they reached the conclusion that mice had chewed the wiring. Something may have been triggered by use of the appliances.

Assistance began to arrive from all over Canada. We went as planned to the CBM retreat, and were lovingly surrounded by "family." Virginia describes the strange experience of having to wait until everyone else had put on their winter clothing. She had been given a coat, mittens, toque, scarf and boots, but couldn't remember what any of them looked like. She had to wait to see what was left.

A little event at that retreat illustrated how easy it is to lose perspective on values. I found a quarter in the coin return slot of the pay phone. My immediate reaction was, "Oh look, I've found a quarter," as if that were a significant event. We were alive, having escaped from a fire, and were immediately receiving gifts that really were significant. Using three categories of resources we were able to rebuild, ending up with a much more adequate house than we had before. We used generous gifts from family and friends all across Canada. We used the proceeds from insurance, even though there were frustrations in arriving at a settlement, and we took out an additional mortgage.

The invasion of my immediate family by three cases of brain cancer within a three-year period was a different kind of cross to bear. The impact of those diagnoses and deaths did not strike fully until well after the last of the three had passed. Certain words, when we encounter them personally, strike fear into our hearts. One of those words, when it relates to those we dearly love, is cancer. The fear intensifies as one comes to grips with the sense of helplessness that accompanies the diagnosis of branches of cancer that do not have a history of responding well to surgery or other treatment.

The name *glioblastoma multiforme* now carries that kind of impact for me and for many of my extended family. It meant nothing when I first heard it in relation to my only sister, Shirley Pickett, on that day in June 1993. Shirley soon underwent brain surgery, which was reported as totally successful at the time, yet by November of that year she was gone. When my mother was diagnosed with the same form of brain cancer in November 1994 this began to look like something more than mere coincidence. Her funeral was in May of 1995. In May of 1996 my only brother, Donald, experienced the same fearful symptoms, and he too was diagnosed as having *glioblastoma multiforme*. By then it had become evident that we were dealing with a concentration in one nuclear family and a frequency of occurrence of a particularly vicious form of cancer that was radically different from the norms of our society.

In each of my family members the malignancy took a slightly different form, as if emphasizing the *multiforme* component of its name. In each the location was different. The location of Donald's malignancy made it inoperable. He had the best alternative treatment available at the time, but in the end his passing was less than seven months from the time that the first clear evidences appeared.

One morning following Mother's brain surgery, when it had become evident that she was again deteriorating rapidly, brother Donald and I visited her at her home in Moncton. Adrenalin permits wonderful moments of strength even when the body is deteriorating. Mother turned to meet us with a smile, sitting higher and more confidently than I had seen her for days. Her speech was a very short one.

"You know, this is our last visit together." In fact, it was the last visit the three of us were to have. And there were few individual visits after that. She was slipping fast, and she definitely welcomed her home-going. We read a psalm of comfort together as she slipped back down into the slumped pose in which she would sleep away much of her remaining few days.

The waves of news signalling these diagnoses and deaths rolled in like breakers from a storm at sea, and with a relentless crescendo of fury. Each of us who related to these loved ones struggled to come to grips with news, with reality, with what seemed like unreality, each with our own spiritual and emotional resources and those that others brought to us. Often it seemed as though the world's clock had stopped in mid-pulsation. Time stood still, and we were in a dazed, suspended animation. Never was it easy. Yet there, in the background, and often in the foreground, this same grace of God, of which I have been writing, was a very real force sustaining life, sustaining hope, assisting the next step.

In my own case, all three deaths were in the background by a number of months when the full impact of grief swelled over me. I was alone in the house at the time, a dull February day with overcast skies, surrounded by the silence that I sought and needed. I was sitting in my recliner chair, a notepad in my lap, reaching for concepts and components that would become part of this volume I'm now writing. I found myself weeping quietly, without knowing why. I wasn't even reviewing the events related to the deaths in my family, for I was working on a different chapter at the time.

Grief had caught up to me. Although I continued to go through the motions of daily life and its duties, I was, in effect, immobilized for weeks. During this time the hymns I carry in memory became a particular source of strength, fortified by Scripture reading and by time spent in prayer, fortified by family and loving friends.

At various points in our career we have ministered to refugees, both in Africa and in Europe. Having been through war, evacuation, fire and loss of loved ones ourselves, those experiences equipped us in part to understand, indeed to empathize with, those who have lost all. Yet we readily acknowledge one immense difference between our situation and theirs. We were surrounded by a loving community with resources. For most of them their communities and their families have also been demolished in the devastation of war. By God's grace we had accessible resources and were able to make a new start. Many of them have nobody and nowhere to turn.

There is no single approved, successful or peaceful way of coming to grips with either the initial blows of a tragedy or with the waves of pain and other emotions that follow. Realization, despondency, grief, accompanied by a whole gamut of other negative sentiments push in and would take over. The amazing grace of God is displayed and experienced in too great a variety of situations, circumstances and people to permit categorization or the construction of simplistic formulae with the suggestion that if one proceeds in a certain way then a particular form of relief can be expected. But this grace of God offers the hope for which we may reach out when it is needed. This may be in the moment of panic, pain, distress, fear, grief or disaster. The accessibility of this grace is well expressed in a portion of the Bible which emphasizes that Jesus, because of his humanity and his own suffering, is very understanding of our own:

> For we do not have a high priest who is unable to sympa-
> thize with our weaknesses, but we have one who has been
> *tempted* in every way, just as we are yet was without sin. Let
> us then approach the throne of grace with confidence, so that
> we may receive mercy and find grace to help us in our time
> of need.

(Hebrews 4:15 & 16, NIV)

The emphasis in the quotation is my own, calling attention to the word translated into English as "tempted." That word can be as easily translated as "tested," implying that with each testing the options of victory or failure are present. In all of our times of testing we may reach out, through Jesus, for this grace of God that is available to sustain us.

It seems as though a forty-year period of my life has consisted of one continuous interaction with "testings" in the form of threats, uncertainty, fear and other external conditions which, for the most part, were beyond personal control. It helped, perhaps, to have grown up on a small farm, close to the land, personally aware of the struggle our family faced to survive in the 1930s. From my parents and grandparents I learned that life itself consists of confronting obstacles, and finding ways either to overcome them or to live with them without being personally overcome. I saw their religious faith make a difference.

My parents and grandparents were also people who acknowledged that in this world God created, death itself constitutes an integral part of the processes of life. The eternal life promised and made available by God begins here and now, where we start to participate in it. Life continues as a reality beyond the grave. Seen in that perspective, death is a transition. That transition is painful and traumatic for all involved, just as birth is painful and traumatic for the mother as well as for the less-than-conscious child. The pain and trauma do not negate the necessity, or even the victory of both death and birth. They are not to be avoided.

6
India
Communication is what is heard

For someone with both cultural and linguistic experience I did not do well on my first visit to India. India's major languages all have their own distinctive scripts. The tribal languages were reduced to writing more recently, using a phonetic script, and are more user friendly for westerners. I carried with me a resolve to listen to the language, make notes in my own phonetically adjusted script, and attempt to seek the meaning of what I perceived to be the key words.

Having recently come to my position as general secretary of Canadian Baptist Ministries, this visit was part of a world tour to become familiar with all aspects of the work in Asia and South America. That first visit began with a stay in Telugu country, along the middle range of India's eastern coastline on the Indian Ocean. With a series of prolonged welcome speeches and a few sermons to sit through, my pen and trusty notebook were at hand, working on linguistic analysis. As I listened, I was convinced that a certain word, which I transcribed as *entwenti,* must be absolutely crucial either to the language or to theology. It topped my list of most frequently used words in Telugu vocabulary. Wrong. That's what a speaker says when he is pondering what to say next, something like "Aaaaah." The rest of my guesses registered about the same degree of significance. In view of the complexity of the Telugu writing system, plus the travel and work pressures associated with the assignment, serious linguistics went by the board.

Worship in the church at Kakinada. Shoes remain outside. Seating on benches or mats is optional.

On then to cross-cultural understanding, which has always been a major interest and concern. The Convention of Baptist Churches of the Northern Circars District had invited me, based in Toronto at the time, to bring four keynote addresses at their annual assembly meetings. The topic was to be stewardship. I agreed and set out to prepare biblical messages that would overcome once and for all that obstacle that plagues every western visitor to India—misunderstanding. There could be no problems and no misunderstandings. Each point would be so very simple, so clear and transparent, with adequate repetition and illustration, that no misunderstanding would be possible. If there was misunderstanding it cannot be laid at the feet of my translator, Rev. T.J. Venkataratnam, who handled the task most admirably.

My first message was based on the biblical premise that we are caretakers of all that God has entrusted to us—we will be held accountable to him for that stewardship. He is the true master of all, but he assigns us responsibilities and entrusts us with resources. The other three messages carried through with the implications of the first. After the four messages had been carefully and very deliberately presented, I was approached by Hugh McNally, who inquired whether I would like to know how I was being interpreted. Hugh's ease with the language made it a simple matter for him to sit with the back-benchers and pick up the drift of their conversations and analyses.

Hugh began with the first message on stewardship, relaying some overall comments to the effect that this man with a Ph.D. must surely have something more profound to say than what was surfacing.

"Aha, we have it. He has also been talking about transferring all the properties to our Convention. So his real message is this—the real owner is still the Canadian Baptist Mission. We are only stewards, and must give a good accounting to the mission, or we will be called into judgement."

Hugh had parallel interpretations for each of the other messages, and I came as close to real depression as I have been through an entire career. If it were not possible with good intentions and deliberate effort to communicate in simplicity with these my brothers in the faith, then what value is there in my being here, and what hope for the future?

Hugh's advice was most pragmatic.

"Cheer up, there's nothing you can do or say that will alter the initial interpretation of these messages. But note too that they have evaluated you as something of a snake, which in this society is a high compliment. Live with it."

Hugh had an additional suggestion as to style.

"Whatever may be your conclusion or your main point, don't come right out and state it directly. Lead toward it and hint at it, then back off. Come with a different approach from a different direction and hint at it again. Allow the hearers to word your conclusions for you, to frame them in their own minds." That was a very helpful point, though I could have wished Hugh had been familiar with a Kikongo proverb: "Teach your child on the way to the market, not on the way home."

Regional gatherings such as this one near Vuyyuru are often
held outside under the temporary pandal erected for shade.

Those properties that my listeners thought I was talking about were to
be a major concern for several visits to come. The property holdings of
Canadian Baptist Ministries were vast, and fell into four general categories. The network of hospital/clinic properties included three hospitals in
Andhra State where we carried full administrative responsibility, plus a
medical outpost at Serango in Orissa State, which was something less
than a full hospital. Different kinds of relationships existed with a couple of other facilities.

A second category would be the educational institutions, ranging from
prestigious high schools that had helped to shape modern India, to little-
known village schools by the dozens. The variations included boarding
facilities for boys and carefully supervised residential schools for girls.
The management of the schools was often a contentious issue, with considerable controversy about who managed, who was on staff and who
was admitted.

The third category of property consisted of what had been the missionary residences, termed "bungalows." That name threw me because I thought I knew what a bungalow was. My grandparents had lived in a bungalow consisting of two small rooms and a porch, with two even smaller bedrooms. The Indian bungalow was something different, built with ample space and high ceilings to cope with tropical heat. These property holdings were vast.

The fourth category of property was the church holdings, places of worship. In reality these four categories of property were often linked in mix-and-match combinations, to baffle any attempt at simplicity.

The CBM purpose, as resolved in Toronto, was to transfer property title deeds to the Convention of Churches, preferably selling non-functional properties and leaving the proceeds in India to help maintain those that were transferred. There was much suspicion that proceeds from sales would be clawed back to Toronto, but this did not happen. Negotiations were met with constant accusations that we were attempting to sell away their birthright. In the end settlements were reached, and agreements signed, but not easily.

Life would be simpler—and Christian witness more effective—if everyone were to interpret terms such as "Christian" and "Baptist" in their truest and more limited sense, but the pressures of the world we live in do not facilitate that. An example of how it worked out in India would be the hypothetical, wayward son of an active, committed Christian family worshipping in the Baptist tradition. This hypothetical son would insist on his right to describe himself as Christian and Baptist. His argument would be based both on exclusion (he is neither Hindu, Muslim, nor Sikh) and association. He would assert proudly that he was born into a Christian family. Just as proudly, he has his diplomas from schools identified by everyone as Christian and Baptist. His identity, as he perceives it, is not tied to active, current affiliation with a church. Furthermore, his neighbours in village, town or city would insist that yes, he is certainly a Christian and a Baptist, and this would be without regard to conduct, church affiliation or even criminal record. Carrying this logic to its next step, these properties under discussion he considers to be his clear birthright. In this he would insist that his conduct, his church membership or

Dr. A. B. Masilamani, standing, became known all over India. Practices related to caste changed in his lifetime.

lack of it, his relationship with God and the rest of the Christian community are irrelevant. These two differing uses of terminology were raised, discussed, and struggled with at all levels, but without resolution.

The influence India exerts upon the church competes seriously with the influence of the church on India. That should not come as a surprise, since this contaminating influence of society on church happens in Canada, the U.S.A. and Europe, as elsewhere. What linguist Don Larson refers to as monocultural myopia impedes our insights on how this force is at work in our own society. Most criticisms that I hear of the church are not levelled at the biblical model of the church, but at the Indian church as contaminated by society and by other additions, human traditions and influences. This observation would hold true for most criticisms levelled at the church on every continent, and certainly in my own country.

In my visits to India I encountered many expressions of warmth, kindness and consideration from total strangers, people without church connections. One of those incidents happened in the airport at Bombay when a recent fire had put the control tower out of commission. There was considerable delay in landing, then the confusion in the airport itself was horrendous. The reservations system and various signs of order had mostly vanished.

It became clear that in order to board the flight to Hyderabad one must have a rubber stamp from a certain kiosk that had been set up in the departures hall. It was utterly mobbed, and I was standing on the outer fringes of the mob. A passenger approached, palms together in the courteous lotus position, and addressed me apologetically.

"Excuse me sir, but there is no other way."

I didn't understand his meaning until he placed his hands against my back and catapulted me through and over a number of other passengers, insisting that I hold out my tickets to be stamped. Mission accomplished, this kind man apologized profusely for his conduct and disappeared in the crowd. Over the years the grace of God in providing solutions to difficult situations has been shown in a great variety of forms. That appearance in Bombay was just one in a series.

The Hyderabad that was our destination is in India's Andhra State, but there is another Hyderabad—in Pakistan, which Virginia and I were to discover abruptly in the middle of the night. Our series of flights had begun in Kenya, but the itinerary and the ticketing had been done in Toronto, by a travel agent who was unaware that there were two cities named Hyderabad.

We arrived in Karachi well after midnight, and the first clue of a problem should have been the instructions to go over to the "internal flights" area of the terminal. There we learned that we were ticketed to fly to Hyderabad in Pakistan. But the flight we needed to connect with was from Hyderabad in India to Visakhapatnam. We were drowsy but rapidly coming awake. We eventually reached a solution by buying a set of tickets from Karachi to Hyderabad (India). We had only recently acquired an American Express Credit Card, and it was accepted by Pakistani airlines. It is disconcerting to face a serious problem far from home, in the middle of the night, in an area where there is no one we can consult for help.

The India which I experienced was an essentially peaceful country where there was little fear of violence in the run of everyday life, apart from those public disturbances when political issues are being raised (if not settled). Remarkable is the country where even thieves are polite— and non-violent.

Waldo Penner, a CBM missionary who has spent his life in India, is a man with an ample frame and a gentle nature. He tells of a night-time experience on the flat roof of his house at Chelligoda. His family was away at the time, and Waldo took a camp cot out to sleep on the roof

Doctors Janaki (with documents) and Susheela managed two hospitals in the CBM network. These remarkable Christian women made a profound impact.

under the stars, to escape the oppressive heat. As Waldo tells it, he awoke in the night to a sound of movement. He may even have seen a moving form. He called out, "Who is it?" The reply he got would have been given only in India. Palms together in the lotus greeting, the frail form replied, "I'm a thief, sir." As Waldo tells it (with a smile), he himself was covered only by a thin sheet. Gathering that sheet around him with one hand and trying to hold it in place, Waldo held the respectful thief's wrist in his other ample hand. Perhaps he gave too much attention to edging the sheet into an appropriate drape. In any event, as they were descending the outside stone staircase, the thief simply launched himself off into thin air at a point near the bottom, and of course he was gone.

The phrase "honour among thieves" may or may not have special reference to India. Ken Knight, CBM treasurer in India, answered my question about the meaning of the name carried by an aspiring young car assistant. "Oh, *Paidi Raju* simply means 'King of the thieves.'" I tried to think of any conceivable situation on another continent where parents would grace their child with such a label. The secret must be to try to readjust one's thinking to find honour in remarkable places.

Try that one on in response to a physician's prominent street sign with the sub-title "M.D. failed" after the physician's name. It seems that this credential appeals to a clientele that is happy to be cared for by a person with the same training as an accredited medical doctor, but who must offer services at a considerably lower rate. Following this same logic across the entire professional scene, one may set up special tutoring with a B.Ed. failed, be defended in court by an Ll.B failed, arrange an audit by a C.A. failed, and so on. There are pastors whose card may indicate B.D. failed, and this would not carry any particular stigma. The phenomenon seems to show itself all up and down the academic scale. There is surely something to be said for a society that adjusts its expectations to provide honourable employment for so many different variations of academic achievement.

One of the personality weaknesses I readily acknowledge has to do with a general lack of patience with people and situations when at home in Canada. Virginia discovered with considerable surprise that this seems to be adjusted somehow when travelling overseas. One situation comes to mind where patience paid off.

Ken Knight and I had travelled to New Delhi with business to transact at the Canadian consulate. Hotel reservations were not normally required, and we had arrived on short notice and late at night, taking our chances. Some special event was underway and the little hotels seemed to be full. We found the reception desk of one of the larger hotels faced with a lineup of vocal and demanding clients. Settling on a sofa in the service manager's line of vision, we sported our best laid-back attitude, catching his eye on one or more occasions, then getting to speak with him.

"We're not in a hurry; we'll be glad to wait over here until you've dealt with all the rest. Would you have some corner for us?" The reply was a grateful affirmative. Over the course of the next hour and more we came to identify individual travellers who returned periodically to pester the help, often with the same phrases: "But I have a reservation." "Sir, I am your regular and honoured guest here." "What about my case?"

When all were finally looked after and the queue had disappeared, a grateful service manager asked that we follow him to the largest room that either Ken or I had ever slept in. Two ballrooms existed side by side in this vast hotel, and the sliding doors were open between them. The staff brought in roll-away cots for us. Unfortunately the check-list we made that night has been lost over the years. We chalked a tally of how many crystal chandeliers lit our vast makeshift bedroom, how many leather sofas, how many original large oil paintings graced our quarters, and all for no extra charge.

The biggest single factor that faith in Jesus as Lord brought to the social fabric of India may well be the dimension of hope in a society where fatalism carries such an impact. Those who are without hope either for the present life or for a future existence have very little indeed. One who has hope grasps present resources, whatever they are, and rearranges them in experimental combinations that result in improved living conditions, in ways that will provide stepping stones for children and other family as well as for self. Someone convinced that fate has destined him or her to conditions that are inalterable ends up frozen in a crippling immobility which, in terms of life outlook, is death in itself.

During a train ride to the northern part of Andhra I was travelling alone and wanted to be left alone to my personal struggle with what I perceived to be weaknesses in the church, springing from weaknesses in individual Christians. A man roughly my age kept attempting to engage me in conversation. He was well dressed, carried himself with confidence and had an aura of culture about him. He pressed for information on my nationality, my reason for visiting India and my profession. Somewhat apologetically, I shared each of these in turn, mumbling an apology that the church body I was dealing with was less than encouraging, and that the institutional church in each country often fails to live up to the ideals of the Christian Scriptures, which we hold dear. Details of that conversation are now faint. I may even have been apologetic that it is such a long journey before converts from the unscheduled castes reach some internationally acceptable standard of public behaviour. The inner concerns with which I was struggling had to do with court cases, struggles for power, and responsible stewardship of funds, with appropriate accounting.

My fellow traveller was not a Christian and was quick to acknowledge that he was speaking about the Christian church as an outsider. He insisted that the perspective I had been sharing with him was totally inappropriate.

"Sir, you are wanting perfection and you look at the flaws. We who have lived here for generations see things differently. In our tradition those people you have been talking about were less than human. They were not even counted as people in India's census. Now we have been made to see that they are real people, they are human. They now participate in politics at the national level and they make a contribution to our nation. You see the flaws but we see how remarkably far that they have come."

This was an unsolicited testimonial. To this day I believe that this man was God's unsolicited expression of his grace to a weakened and discouraged person. It often happens. Though it might be a temptation for Christians to think that God would choose to work and speak only through an obedient and responsive believer, the biblical record establishes a different principle. The prophets Isaiah (44:28 & 45:1) and Jeremiah (25:9) are both mouthpieces of God announcing this reality. With Jeremiah it is a very striking declaration, in unequivocal terms: *This is what the Lord Almighty, the God of Israel says: I will send for my servant Nebuchadnezzar, king of Babylon, and I will set his throne over these stones* (Jeremiah 43:10, NIV).

From time to time I had graphic glimpses of just how far India had come in as little as one generation. Dr. A. B. Masilamani was a living testimony to this. He tells of how his father, shepherding animals, first brought a search for light and truth into their family. One day the wind tumbled a random piece of paper across the fields, dropping it to rest near the shepherd's feet. The paper had markings on it. The shepherd,

Dr. Masilamani's father, took this paper to someone who could read. It was part of the story of Jesus. That began a search to learn the rest of the story, but the story itself has no ending. Those who have been brought by "Masi" to this new and revolutionary way of living and of relating to God in Jesus, continue today to tell others.

A cameo of history, truly revolutionary in nature, surfaced as Masi and I were driving through a certain village. It turned out that in 1932, the year I was born, the very man who became known around the world as Dr. A. B. Masilamani, teacher and evangelist, had been stoned for daring to ride a bicycle. Here, on this very street. This act was considered to be audacious to the point of outrage. That someone from an unscheduled caste would do such a thing! What did he think he was . . . a human being? India has come so far, and so many heroes have contributed. Some of those who brought about such changes in India are people who called Jesus their Lord.

At the other end of the social scale were those who sacrificed inheritance, love, family, reputation and every human advantage for the privilege of worshipping God as revealed through Jesus. Late at night I listened to the personal family history of those whose father's declaration of faith meant first that they were denied water at the well, then food at the table, then any part of a vast inheritance. The many who made sacrifices of this nature tended not to talk about anything lost. Their emphasis was on what they had gained.

Our Canada is one of those post-Christian countries in which it has become quite normal to meet the observation that what one believes really doesn't matter in everyday life. Pragmatically, religious belief is considered to be irrelevant. India is a country where it can be demonstrated that beliefs make a very real difference in everyday life.

During my visits to India in the 1970s, conventional wisdom had it that approximately seventy percent of the food produced in India was lost to a combination of rodents and bad storage. Because of these factors, a country that had the capacity to feed itself was unable to do so, and was therefore an importer of food. Because of the prevailing religious belief that after death a person could be reborn into a lower form of animal life, animals were not killed—and that included rats. In effect, the result was that rat control in such a densely populated country was little more than a rat exchange on some glorious scale. Rats were trapped, taken far and released. But what is far from one person's home is near to that of someone else. In addition to food wastage there is the consideration of rats and their fleas as carriers of deadly disease.

India has changed and is changing. The subcontinent has an impressive depth of both history and culture. Given its complexity and the staggering population of more than a thousand million people, the rate of change is quite phenomenal. Along the roads of Andhra state in 1970 one would meet what seemed like endless lines of oxcarts, often carrying sugar cane to refineries. Two phenomena led me to take special note of the technology. First, I was the son of the Canadian farm, and brought a lot of curiosity to the experience. Second, there was a peculiar, high-pitched squeak to the wheel of an oxcart turning on a wooden axle. I discovered that by far the majority of the carts were using wooden axles at that time, as they had done for generations. After all, tradition has it that Ashoka was the inventor of the wheel. India's flag carries the wheel as its reminder to the world of this invention central to world technology and the age of machines. By 1980 that age-honoured technology had almost totally given way in coastal Andhra to the metal axle, so much stronger, more efficient and easy to lubricate.

It was Gordon Carder, another CBM career missionary who has devoted his life to India, who introduced me to a partnership in driving as experienced nowhere else in the world. Gordon had a sporty little black roadster convertible with no electric horn. Its replacement was actually more convenient to the Indian milieu as long as there was a fellow passenger, as the horn was located on the passenger side. Before he started the motor Gordon gave me my instructions. Whenever the motor was running I was to keep squeezing the large rubber bulb, which issued a blaring honk—all day if necessary. I was free to stop only when the engine stopped. The reason for this tied in with the lines of oxcarts that we would be passing all the way to our destination. Drivers of the oxcarts would be asleep on the tongue of the cart, between their oxen. The oxen, at the sound of a distant horn, begin in their unhurried, ambling way to move toward the edge of the road, leaving room to pass. If the passenger fails in his honking, the result is stoppage behind an oxcart blocking the road. When the remiss passenger does begin honking, no matter how impatiently, the move to the edge is not faster or slower; it only begins later because there was no advance notice.

It was a special privilege to travel with Stan Boulter in India, and to note how he thought and how he worked. A businessman from Vancouver who had managed coconut oil plantations in the Pacific, Stan had also visited India in 1957 with the trade commission from Canada which at the same time established Canada's High Commission in that subcontinent. On one of my trips to India Stan accompanied me in the capacity of a board member from CBM, and the two of us were equipped with a "power-to-act" mandate that would facilitate the transfer of properties to India-based entities. Stan was a man of utter integrity, vast experience and perceptive insights.

Apprenticeship begins at an early age for young businessmen. This can be anywhere from seven to eight years of age upward. As Stan Boulter and I approached the airport at Madras, Stan commented that he had experienced about enough of decrepit airport buses.

"Why don't we take a taxi to the Connemara this time?"

There, in the arrival lobby just beyond baggage claims, a young entrepreneur was ready for us.

"Reliable taxi, sir?"

"Yes, son. We'll have a reliable taxi."

Before one could blink, this little bundle of sinew had two bags on his head, and was trotting on ahead, ours the responsibility of keeping him in view. For just such a purpose I had decorated all sides of my luggage with self-adhesive, fluorescent red dots. They helped in keeping one's luggage in view. That worked fine until one day I noted enterprising airport personnel in Bombay putting them in the middle of their foreheads, probably for their wives at home.

Back to our young entrepreneur, who was now way out ahead. He had passed the regular line of authorized airport taxis and was headed for a private parking lot somewhere down along the runway. Our luggage was waiting for us beside a black antique of dubious vintage, which appeared to have had a park bench put in to replace the worn out original seat. It was covered with black plastic to match the trim, all very *pukkah*.

We negotiated our fare to the Connemara, only marginally greater than the bus fare. It was then we discovered multiple reasons why all the extra personnel were hovering around. First, it seems the owner was ill and our ten-year-old was on hand to instruct the rookie driver on the many secrets of how this automobile might run, if all signs were auspicious. Three of the extras were there to push, in the absence of a starter. Our start out through the airport gate was rather promising in spite of coughings, wheezings and a rough clutch. Just beyond the airport gate something happened in or near the engine that sounded remarkably like an explosion. All movement ground to a halt under a black cloud of smoke. We as passengers were not expected to help push the vehicle to the edge of the road, and anyway that happened in short order. There were excited exchanges in Tamil.

As we sat there a shiny, new and beautiful airport bus passed us on its way to the Connemara and downtown. No comments from either Stan or John, but I think I noted considerable tension in a set of jaw muscles. A series of other taxis were flagged, with additional avid conversation in Tamil. You see, we were operating on a negotiated fare, and our own reliable taxi required its share of the profit, regardless of the mechanical breakdown. Eventually we got to the Connemara in this second, also reliable, taxi. By then the airport bus and its passengers were nowhere in sight.

Another taxi event, starting this time from the Bangalore airport, could have turned out to be a more ugly experience. Virginia and I were travelling together and we had not heard about the strike action underway there in an attempt to tie up public transportation. Nothing public was supposed to be functioning—no buses, no taxis. Our flight into Bangalore had been remarkably empty. Obviously others knew what was happening even if we didn't.

Visits to rural areas of India could involve travel on foot.

We landed, picked up our luggage and proceeded outside to find the unusual situation of no taxis in sight, reliable or otherwise. We still didn't know why. Eventually a taxi driver arrived. He may have seemed furtive, or is that my imagination after the fact? He insisted on a price that seemed high, but there were no alternatives available. What happened next was over so quickly that there was no chance to analyze what was taking place. Our driver topped a hill and there before us were several hundred strikers, complete with banners, spread across both halves of the boulevard, which had a grass strip in the middle. It was a downhill run to where they were massed. Our driver floored the accelerator, headed straight at them with whatever speed he could muster. The shouting and waving of fists had already begun, but with immediate evidence that they were parting to let us through. It was for just such an eventuality that the strikers had gathered piles of sizeable rocks.

We have never travelled light. Being functional with an office on the road was always more important than light luggage. In those days, in addition to check-in bags, there was always a portable Olympia type-writer in one hand, with a black bag of imitation leather slung over the other shoulder. In the taxi we held these in our laps. The typewriter went up against the window on my side; Virginia held the black bag to the window on her side. Our adventurous driver had his window down, and was now running his vehicle at top speed directly at the group blocking the road. At the last minute he held the car straight on course and lowered his head below the level of the window.

The thundering of rocks against the car lasted only seconds, then we were through. I looked back to glimpse the very incarnation of human rage and indignation. We were out of their reach, however, and headed for Bangalore. No other barricades were in sight. Our driver informed us that he would not be able to go to the hotel that had been recommended—but he had a cousin who owned a hotel. We agreed to go there.

At his cousin's modest hotel we got out to pay the fee and survey the damage. Suddenly there was a tantrum of pretended indignation.

"Look! Look at my car! You must pay." The same thought had already occurred to me, but the driver and I had arrived at remarkably different estimates. Going for damage control I weakly commented that the car wasn't exactly new when we got into it. The reply was quite unexpected.

"But you must pay me at least five extra rupees."

That would be equivalent to less than a dollar at the time. Being such a generous spender, I gave him four times what he had asked. He blessed us and departed, happy as a lark. I suspect he was not the owner; nor would the owner ever see the extra twenty rupees.

We had not been deliberate strike breakers, but that stoning represented a very real peril, given the speed of the vehicle, the angry tenor of the mob and their pile of rocks at the ready. Looking back over four decades of close calls, this one very definitely ranks among the remarkable instances where we sensed the hand of God demonstrably caring for us. The Psalm has distinctive meaning which reads this way:

> *I trust in you, O Lord;*
> *I say, "You are my God,*
> *My times are in your hands."*

> Psalm 31:14 & 15, NIV

In a dozen or more visits to India I experienced various unsettling incidents of public protest. On one occasion our car was manhandled repeatedly by a crowd of students who had blocked the road with poles and railway ties, calling for the repeal of certain rules relating to a region around Hyderabad. Angry faces pressed against the glass, but we passengers were not pulled out. Although the rocking and the shouted threats were tense, the protesters stopped short of overturning the car and did not set it on fire. On another occasion the track had been torn up and our train could not proceed. No injury came from either of these incidents.

During an overnight train ride Virginia and I took from Vijayawada to Madras a group of local bootleggers forced their way on board and settled in the hallway of our wagon. It was obvious that they were going to drink much of the profit from what they had intended to sell in the city. An anxious railway attendant knocked on our door, identified himself, and came in to apologize. Employees on the train were not numerous enough to establish order.

"Sir, you must believe me that this never happens on our train. It will certainly be corrected in Madras."

We were to lock our door and not open it under any pretext before arrival. It was an uneasy night with short intervals of sleep punctuated by pounding on our door, singing, shouting and arguments carried on in loud, drunken voices. Sunrise came just before the train slowed at the Madras platform. Police had been called and were there in force, emptying our hallway in an instant. The rising sun projected the shadow of the train against the walls of buildings to the west. We could see clearly the profiles of police in chase along the top of the train, swinging their *lathis* at the culprits, who seemed to be sobering rapidly.

There have been popular accusations that Christian missions operated in India under the protection of the British colonial government and were assisted by favours from that government. No evidence of favour or protection surfaced in the dozen or so visits that I paid to India, and I was deliberately alert to that issue. Nevertheless, with the passing of decades, and with the maturing of Christian leadership capacity, it was becoming imperative that a new and different style of mission-church relationship be brought into being, whether or not it was universally popular.

CBM invested much prayer and energy in attempting to bring about the transition that would free the church and its institutions for service in a new era. This topic absorbed more energy than any other topic of interaction among us. It was not possible to avoid hard feelings and conflict, though that conflict never became violent. Sizeable and influential institutions were involved. Specifically these were hospitals, schools, places of worship and the denominational infrastructures.

That struggle to achieve an appropriate post-colonial style of mission-church relationship is not within the scope of this volume, but the following remarks do seem appropriate:

• There was great diversity of conviction within CBM's resident missionary community, along with a similar divergence in the emerging Indian leadership. This made it difficult to arrive at anything like consensus.

• Where differences existed involving individual convictions, those convictions were based on sincerity and a desire to do the will of God.

• As one directly involved, I derived a considerable sense of rightness and conviction from the unity in policy and direction that existed among CBM's executive staff. The same is to be said about unity between staff and the directors who established that policy and direction.

- The grace of God is as important a factor in carrying us through relational perils as it is in caring for us in the midst of physical perils.

7
Bolivia
Blood still cries out

A certain sadness hangs over my associations with Bolivia. This probably springs from my working visit in 1977, when I learned of the death of my father and was not even able to communicate with my family back in Canada.

I was travelling with Rev. Mel Ralston, who was a CBM board member at the time. Mel and I had crossed one ridge of the Andes from Cochabamba in the central valley to the tropical rain forest along the Chapare River. The Bolivian Baptist Union operated a medical clinic near one of its churches there.

The beginnings of the clinic are mostly associated with the name of Dr. Margaret Cserepka and her husband John. This delightful couple had escaped from Hungary in 1956, when the popular uprising against the Communist regime was crushed by Russian tanks. Through their terms of service the Cserepkas made a lasting impact on the population, who recognized in them the love of Jesus. At the time of our visit the clinic, which was often something of a field hospital, was efficiently and appropriately operated by Dr. Quispe.

It was a March visit, late summer in Bolivia, the seasons being reversed south of the equator. Rains were heavy at the time and, although we got safely into the Chapare, an enormous landslide wiped out the road behind us. The Chapare clinic, like many remote outposts, was

This landslide on the road to the Chapare Valley blocked traffic for several days at the time of a death in the family (also next two photos).

equipped with a short wave radio transceiver. These sets give technical problems from time to time. That week the clinic was able to receive messages but not transmit.

I received a message announcing my father's death in Salisbury, New Brunswick. The family had set a tentative funeral date, and they were waiting for my response to see if I would be able to come. Not only was I unable to travel, I couldn't even send a return message. This complicated arrangements for Mother, Virginia and other family members. In view of my silence they were unsure whether to proceed with the funeral or to delay, hoping I might send word or even be on my way home. In the end they did proceed with the funeral and I was grateful for their sound judgement.

The loneliness of the next two or three days of grief was intensified by the isolation and the frustration of not even being able to send a message. Having a Canadian pastor travelling with me was a wonderful as-

set. Additional comfort came from a surprising corner. Dr. Quispe, single and a number of years younger than I, carried the kind of heart that reached out to mine, across barriers of culture and language, in a way that I never would have imagined possible.

That was not the first landslide on that mountain road, nor the last. The Bolivian road services move heavy equipment to the trouble spots and proceed with road repair. In a few days we received word that it was now possible to leave by road, which we did. The bulldozers were there, creating a new and usable single track across a vast, sloping area where layers of rock from above had been loosened by the rain.

I made another memorable visit to the same Chapare area, this time in a Cessna plane—even though Chapare had no airstrip. It worked this way. Radio communication from Cochabamba confirmed that the Cserepka vehicle was in working order and gave our estimated time of arrival. Our pilot, Ivan Pettigrew, circled the Chapare clinic once or twice and verified that Pastor John had indeed taken the Toyota to one end of a straight stretch of road and positioned it strategically to stop any oncoming traffic. A clinic helper had been left at the other end of the straight stretch, just by the bridge. We then circled once more to make a straight approach to this fine paved provisional runway.

But a complication developed. A man with a bicycle had just come up onto the road, unaware of our presence, his back to the approaching aircraft, which was very quiet with the motor idled back to landing speed. These little planes are not equipped with horns, and the cyclist was unaware of our approach to the very last minute. Sitting in the front seat beside the pilot, I watched his reactions closely. Should we circle and make another approach? No, there's still enough room to land beyond where he'll be. Ivan idled in at a very low elevation, six to ten meters over the cyclist's head, then dropped the plane softly on the tarmac. When he had braked, Ivan spun the plane to taxi back to a parking spot. This gave me a good view of the cyclist, who was in the process of picking himself and his cycle out of the ditch. There was no opportunity to meet this man or check his reactions, but it is certain that he had an interesting yarn to share with his friends. If we caused him a laundry problem, at least the Chapare River was near at hand.

Ivan Pettigrew was an interesting pilot to fly with, filled with stories of hair-raising events in the mountains and valleys of Bolivia, where the terrain is so unforgiving. I asked if he had ever had to set down in a certain area we were crossing.

"As a matter of fact, I once had to put down on that steep slope you can see over there where some corn or potatoes had been planted." He had repaired a broken steering cable on site. Because of the steeply ramped mountainside he was able to take off downhill out of the garden itself.

"But my passengers got carried away in their evangelization of the local village and didn't get back before the deadline I had set for them. I had to fly out in time to arrive at the Cochabamba airport before dark." It seems his passengers had to find their way out to the highway on foot. After hearing that story, I was constantly on the lookout for sandbars or fields that would serve as emergency landing sites. I learned that Ivan always did the same. Flying out of Cochabamba airport, one can take advantage of a certain side valley to gain altitude. It's an interesting phenomenon to look up and see a shepherd boy tending his sheep or llamas, looking down on the little plane.

On another flight Ivan yawned and informed me that I would be taking over as co-pilot, since he needed a snooze. Although I'm not a pilot, this had happened on a couple of occasions before, and it's an interesting experience. Before pulling his cap down to rest his eyes, Ivan pointed out our passage gap between two of the Andes peaks.

"Remember, you've got to get us up to fourteen thousand feet before we get there, or you're in trouble." A World War II pilot had mentioned to me at some time that their standing orders at that time were not to fly above ten thousand feet without oxygen. We were flying considerably above that, but having taken off from an airport that is eight thousand feet above sea level probably made adjustment easier. The El Alto international airport at La Paz was reported to have one of the longest runways in the world in the 1970s. This is due to the aerodynamic requirements for lift-off at an altitude of 13,000 feet, where the atmosphere is so thin. When taking off from La Paz, passengers get the impression that they must be commuting by land, but eventually the critical speed and lift combination is reached and the plane begins to rise ever so slowly.

Prior to my first world tour as executive officer of CBM I had received many facets of orientation. However, nobody had thought to alert me to the effect of landing at an airport 13,000 feet above sea level. The effects of the altitude alone are enough to merit special care. Specifically, one should move slowly at first, avoid bending over quickly and allow hours, if not days, for the body to adjust to the differences in atmospheric pressure and oxygen content in the blood. Otherwise the symptoms are likely to be nausea, dizziness and shortness of breath. On this first visit during February of 1971 my situation was complicated by fatigue. I had been travelling approximately forty-eight hours without sleep since setting out from Jakarta, Indonesia. The best itinerary my travel agent could find took me on an extended jaunt with stops in Sydney, Pago-Pago, Honolulu, Vancouver, Los Angeles, Lima, La Paz—eight flights without an overnight stopover. There were seven changes of aircraft, with waiting periods built in.

Arrival at La Paz in this state of fatigue was not a good experience. When the cabin doors were opened I immediately felt the pressure in my chest and the shortness of breath that experienced travellers would have been prepared for. When the luggage was delivered I bent over quickly to pick up my two bags, and collapsed in the process. Then under the good care of my hosts I rested, drank coca tea, and recovered appropriately.

One's first visit to a country often leaves the most vivid impressions. Mario Rivas was president of the Baptist Union in 1970. A colourful person in terms of personality, he has a very direct relational style. Years of working in Africa had ingrained an appreciation of the cultural outlook of the Kongo peoples of Angola and Zaire. Theirs were "face-to-face societies," egalitarian cultures with whom Europeans and North Americans can establish relatively easy communications, with understanding and relationships not radically different from those in our own societies. Doctoral studies in anthropology had prepared me in part to accept the differences of varying societies without a judgemental bias, seeking only to understand the differences without classifying one as superior, another inferior.

This background did not remove all the frustrations of trying to come to grips with communications in India, where I had just visited for a number of weeks. In India, try as I might, there was no sense of being able to define exactly where I stood in relation to anyone else. The verbal affirmations in India all insisted that I lived somewhere in the clouds in terms of perfection, wisdom, wondrous largesse, and on and on. The suspicion I held at the end of the first visit was that although these were the affirmations, the opinions might well be quite the opposite.

Mario Rivas quickly defined the Keith relationship to Bolivian Baptists, and later took John to visit with miners.

Coming from India and Indonesia, then flying on from La Paz to Cochabamba, I walked directly into an active session of the Bolivian Baptist Union in full assembly, with Mario Rivas behind the podium. He and others were expecting my arrival, and someone had been delegated to bring me directly from the airport to the session. Before I had even walked down the aisle to the seat waiting for me, President Mario Rivas had defined for me exactly where I stood in this society.

"Welcome, Dr. Keith. Here among us you have a voice; you have no vote." Some Canadians in the assembly later mentioned that they were shocked. Personally, I was delighted.

During that visit I had requested the privilege of staying in the homes of national church leaders when possible rather than with missionaries. This was a bit of a departure from practice, but a rich experience. One facet was more exciting than I had expected. Staying with Mario Rivas and his lovely family in Oruro, I agreed to go with Mario to a meeting requested by church leaders in a nearby mining town. We drove in Mario's jeep. Along the way he seemed to be emphasizing, almost to the extreme, how the outlook of the miners differed from that of other Bolivians. Working in the mines, they live under harsh conditions; they are also constantly exposed to explosives, which seem to be readily available everywhere.

"They solve their problems differently," Mario explained. "A young man disappointed in love will make a belt from explosives, detonate it and kill himself. See that church there? They had a disagreement here in the village. Some were holed up in the church, others threw in dynamite and blew the doors out."

Arriving at our destination, I was led into the strangest circle of Baptist leaders I had ever met. They were rough looking and poorly dressed, but that in itself was not new. Their overcoats were buttoned to the top button in the unheated church. Their feet, rough, purple and shod in sandals made from truck tires seemed oblivious to the cold, but that too was not so different for Bolivia. The difference was that nobody, nobody at all, would look me in the eye. There was a lot of uneasy shuffling of feet until one man brought out a list of what turned out to be seventeen demands, and began to read them. At that point all attention galvanized, and suddenly everyone was looking me in the eye—and all at once.

Now, this scene was playing itself out under less-than-perfect communication conditions. Being a Portuguese-speaker I could mostly understand Spanish. Mario, who speaks Spanish, Brazilian Portuguese and English, helped where necessary. The miners had more difficulty understanding my Portuguese, so Mario helped more in that direction. The miners' chosen spokesman was coming on strong. The Canadian Baptist mission must open certain schools, must put Canadian personnel in certain clinics, must provide certain benefits for the children of miners, must pay the salary of a pastor to be sent here and on and on. We never did get to the end of the list, although I eventually received a copy of the paper.

When the reader got to about point ten or twelve I held up my hand and asked to speak.

"What year is this?" was my question. They couldn't believe the question, so it was repeated verbatim. Puzzled, someone answered, "This is 1971." My reply was that their demands sounded more like something coming out of 1935, before a Bolivian Baptist Union had been formed. They now had Bolivian leaders whom they could choose themselves. Bolivians made the decisions. To agree to the demands would imply a radical return to paternalism, making life difficult for them and their church. I commented that there might be a local Communist cell in their town (the understatement of the year). I asked whether they wanted to leave themselves open to a Communist accusation that their pastor, paid from "the north," must be an agent of imperialism.

From that point the encounter turned into a dialogue that continued for perhaps two more hours and in that time the atmosphere changed radically. Some sense of fellowship emerged, in spite of the confrontational beginning and in spite of the fact that no promises had been secured.

The ride back to Oruro was calmer. There was no longer a need to speak of the violent and different nature of miners.

Some kilometres along we encountered two trucks stopped nose to nose. The drivers were out by the cliff's edge, locked in a savage round of kicking and butting, with fists slamming and blood dripping. Into this fray little Mario Rivas plunged with a fearless vigour that holds my admiration to this day. He became a very pro-active peacemaker, pulling them apart like a referee at a hockey match, but without a helmet. Risking the rage of both, he succeeded in bringing them to a point of shouting instead of fighting. An interpretation of the rules of the road was in dispute. Perhaps more to the point, personal honour and machismo were on the line. Where roads are narrow, right of way needs to be established. Throughout Bolivia, on mountain roads a loaded truck proceeding uphill has uncontested preference. The problem here was that two trucks had met on a level interval just between two areas where the upward bound truck could have insisted on his priority. The situation was somehow resolved and we were allowed to pass.

When we arrived back at the Rivas home in Oruro, Mario's wife Lidia came running, almost shouting her greeting.

"Thank God you're safe."

I asked what she meant by that.

"They didn't take you hostage," she replied. So that's what had been in the works for me! Both she and Mario apparently knew that the stage had been set for these miners to hold me hostage until their demands were negotiated. It seems I missed an opportunity to learn Spanish both earlier and better (living long-term as a hostage) than actually happened over the next seventeen or eighteen years of visits to Bolivia.

On one of those visits I gained personal experience of what hostage-taking could be like, though I was still spared the worst of it. That visit was shortly after I had had knee surgery. Getting around with the use of a cane was workable, though it cramped my personal style. Bolivia was in turmoil that week as a result of a rise in sugar prices. The peasant population, in open defiance of the government and the police, had closed some of the major highways.

Rev. Jaime Goytia was in one of his terms as president of the Bolivian Baptist Union. Jaime knows Bolivia well, and proposed that we undertake a visit to a certain rural church that could be reached by back roads. Marilyn Lemon, Baptist Union treasurer, would need to accompany us. The visit came off successfully and we were within perhaps fifteen kilometres of Cochabamba on our return when we met with a surprise.

I was dozing at the time, Jaime driving the short-wheelbase Toyota Land Cruiser. Coming around a turn, Jaime braked behind a line of stopped vehicles. We were immediately surrounded by a group of armed men who shouted instructions. We must pull up behind the bus ahead, and park for the night. Vehicles and their passengers were being held so that the government would take notice and take corrective action on the price of sugar. No problem; we complied.

The situation seemed humorous for an hour or so, and we settled in to get some rest. Marilyn was given the front seat; Jaime and I attempted to curl up in the back, each of us on a short seat at either side. This involved

Dr. Jaime Goytia, one of Bolivia's outstanding evangelical church leaders, became Latin America Secretary for the United Bible Societies. He shared in our roadblock adventure.

experimenting with knees doubled, knees straight with feet toward the front seat, feet toward the middle, and lots of shifting from time to time. Voices were raised outside periodically, but nothing seemed ominous. As if to prove that we weren't sleeping much, the arrival of each subsequent vehicle brought chuckles from each of us, with comments on the arrival of "another innocent." Something about the whole situation seemed to trigger the giggles, repeatedly, until Jaime's foray outside some time after 4 a.m. He came back changed and totally subdued.

"Many of the peasants are drunk, and they are well armed. The situation is turning ugly. You two Canadians are in much more peril than I am—you would make ideal personal hostages. We must get you out of here around daybreak and before the army arrives. Blood will be spilled here today."

Jaime judged that about daybreak it would still be possible for us to actually walk along the line of vehicles and past the barricade, making

Marilyn Lemon and John Keith escaped from the violence of a roadblock incident in this truck.

our way toward Cochabamba. The worst scenario would be having to walk all the way to Cochabamba. Not the easiest, considering the cane and my healing knee, but better than running the risk of staying. We were not even challenged as we passed the barricade. By then others were following the same tactics.

The strategy probably would have succeeded if the bus driver just arriving from Cochabamba had been willing to wait farther back from the barricade. As it was, he came too close and it was obvious to those manning the barricade that their hostages were escaping. It took a number of minutes to get together their yellow pursuit vehicle, which was some sort of van or panel truck with several logs tied to a roof rack. Apart from his greed, the bus driver would have been able to escape and still make a small fortune with the exorbitant rates he was collecting for this hazardous venture. But he had to stay until the very last of the stragglers had arrived, paid and entered. By then the pursuit vehicle was cranked up and starting. The race was underway. Phase one involved much blowing

Travellers Keith, Lemon and Goytia were held overnight at this roadblock on the road to Santa Cruz. Violence the following day took a number of lives.

of horns, blinking of lights and brandishing of pistols from both front windows of the pursuit vehicle. No surrender. The bus was weak on speed, but in phase two, using his mirrors, the driver was able to weave in front of every effort to pass, whether on the left or on the right. It is doubtful that this endeared him (or any of us) to the pursuit crew.

Phase three came into play as the pursuit vehicle finally passed by cutting out around us through a field. We were in trouble. Our bus was then forced off the road into the field, still travelling at top speed, but quickly coming to a halt. The pursuit crew bailed out of their yellow van, and many scattered in search of rocks. In Bolivia it never takes more than a few steps to locate a convenient throwing rock.

The biblical story of the stoning of Stephen has been part of my memory bank from my childhood, but the mental image carried all those years was quite inaccurate. On the way home from school there was always time for throwing the many stones that had been rolled toward the ditch by the grader. Probably every fence post and telephone pole in that kilo-metre or so between the Keith farm and the school carries the dents of a young boy's efforts to perfect his throwing arm. The road's edge was kept perpetually clean of all stones of throwing size, stones just larger or just smaller than a golf ball, preferably a bit flat to fit in the curve of an index finger. My image of the stoning of Steven involved such stones, but Bolivia convinced me that my impression was way off. These men went for stones that looked more like bowling balls than golf balls. They were dead serious, and they came at the bus well armed and on the run. Two pistols were still in evidence as well. At this juncture the bus driver was totally ready to follow orders, but which orders? One indicated here, another there, another to back up.

Fortunately, in the process the driver opened a door, and we were out of there. How the bus argument ended, and with what degree of punish-ment or payment we never learned. Marilyn and I were already well on our way to the next adventure, swinging leg and cane. Lots of people passed us, for our speed was not up to the demands of the day. From around the next bend a truck approached, the driver receiving copious shouted, urgent instructions from those who had passed us. By the time Marilyn and I reached his turning spot it was a moment to be grasped, for this driver was not going to hang around. The truck bed was probably just below shoulder level. There was no loading ramp or ladder, and there was going to be no assistance from anyone. First I threw my cane and bag on the truck; Marilyn threw her bag. I picked her up and dumped her like a sack of potatoes on the truck bed and was only just able to catch the side racks as the truck revved and departed. We were away with no waiting, passengers all keeping an intent eye on the road behind. Nothing followed us.

Approaching Cochabamba there was a bit of the lighter moment. This was no secret passage we were making. A truck without a muffler can be heard a long distance in every direction. Any driver knows better than to try to make it through the city in such condition, so ours stopped by the side of the road at the city limits and came looking for his muffler. Nei-ther I nor any of the other passengers recognized it but there it was in our midst all along—I would call it a tomato soup can with a long wire at-

Visitors Ernie Ellis (CBM chair) and John Keith (general secretary) were eager to try their hand at the axe when a tree had to be felled to save the Chapare clinic from rampaging flood waters.

tached. He crawled under the truck and slipped this can over the end of his manifold pipe. *Voilà,* a muffler, and the journey continued to where we could get a taxi, then on by taxi to the Baptist centre.

But of course we arrived without Jaime, still back at the roadblock. Toward the end of the day he appeared, in his usual good humour, with his own story to tell. It seems that our Toyota, the most attractive of the 4 x 4 vehicles held hostage, was commandeered by the leader of the block-ade group to forage in the countryside for food. We eventually got it back, perhaps four days later, virtually undamaged.

Jaime's chuckles had to do with the transportation he had arranged. Like us, he had set out to walk to Cochabamba. He met a cyclist with a problem. Too much alcohol, too little balance, but lots of good will. The owner may have been short on balance, but lacked nothing in opinions or determination. They experimented with various combinations, a bit of trial and error with a couple of falls. The only workable solution the owner would accept had Jaime sitting on the crossbar steering while the owner pedalled. At one particularly steep hill Jaime suggested that they might walk. His dramatization of the cyclist exerting his utmost was superb. *"Soy muy macho, soy muy macho,"* he insisted. "I am very macho." That affirmation a passenger was not allowed to contest.

The army did appear that day. Blood did flow, and there were deaths. The newspaper reported four killed. With the appropriate adjustment for official army and police figures, with blending and weighing of local reports, the final estimate was that twenty people must have died where we had spent the night.

This particular visit to Bolivia was crammed with more dramatic events than usual. A mud-slide nearly carried us over a cliff. We screeched to a stop on a mountain road, nose to nose with a bus. There was a shooting event in a village, and more. Lorne Stairs, brother to our long-time colleague Lynn, commented on the series of nine life-threatening events that happened during this one short stay of a few weeks.

"You know, you haven't experienced anything that the rest of us don't go through. But in your case all this has happened at once."

Over the years the Southern Cross Radio station, established by Baptists of Canada, was the special target for violence and capture in revolution after revolution. (In a hundred-and-fifty-year period of its history Bolivia experienced no less than one hundred and eighty distinct revolutions.) Why the Southern Cross Radio? Because it had a history of being careful to broadcast only the truth. Anything less would detract from and undermine its main message of hope and faith and salvation through Jesus Christ. This made it a special target for those who might want to convince the city that all was under their control, when that might not yet be the case. One Canadian Baptist apartment was located over and beside the station. Another house was nearby. From those places I heard the rumble of tanks in the street, enough to realize something of the conditions that colleagues would have experienced under siege.

It is with utter admiration that I consider what CBM personnel have gone through in the century since Archibald Reekie went to Bolivia as the Canadian Baptist pioneer in 1898. Among those were Norman Dabbs and seven Bolivian colleagues who paid the supreme sacrifice at

John Keith, as general secretary of CBM, receives the Bolivian government's highest award, Condor of the Andes, in the degree "Grand Official." Bolivia's minister of education represents President Banzer at the event on November 30, 1973. The award was given to Canadian Baptist Ministries in recognition of 75 years of service to the Republic.

Melchamaya, being stoned to death for their faith in 1949. Two Bolivian eyewitnesses described it to me as an event that shook Bolivia and eventually brought about both political and social change. With those changes came a functional religious freedom in Bolivia.

8
Kenya
Safety and the purposes of God

Across these forty or so years of overseas assignments with Canadian Baptist Ministries I have had serious contact with more than fifteen nations outside North America. Laying aside very important considerations such as friendships, projects, opportunities, assignments and the growth of the church there, Kenya as a country has probably held the strongest attraction and fascination for me. It is a country of nostalgia *par excellence*, with, in the 1970s and '80s, just the right combination of accessibility, communications, and stability to make it an easy place to visit. Those many visits have produced a wealth of memories. It is probably the variety and richness of animal species, especially the profusion of big game, that has its grip on mind and memory. The beauty of the country and the intricacies of widely diverse cultures are a bonus.

Neither adventure nor the attraction of animals played any part in the purpose behind my being in Kenya. Neither of those would have sustained me through the collective months I spent there. More significantly, that kind of motivation would not have sustained the people, both Canadian and Kenyan, who came to be colleagues and fellow-workers. With that qualification, the sense of both adventure and beauty has always run high in connection with Kenyan visits. Kenya's population, animals and panoramas are so diverse, so beautiful and so readily accessible that they are a constant attraction.

Ron and Joan Ward with family in 1980.

Our only period of actual residence in Kenya lasted three and a half months, starting in September 1982. We had two specific purposes. Virginia and I both enrolled in the Kiswahili language learning program run by the Church of the Province of Kenya—Anglican. Mornings were occupied with classroom work. In the afternoons I partnered with a seminary student, Julius Karanja, to fulfil the second purpose. This was to research and prepare an urban ministry survey for the African Christian Church and Schools. Julius has more recently been elected to leadership of this denomination, under the title "dignitary." The study focused on Kenya's main urban centres, especially on the city of Nairobi.

Ethnic conflict in Kenya during the 1980s produced a series of explosive events that affected Canadian Baptist personnel working there. One of those episodes was beginning to unfold during the same week that Virginia and I were stoned at Bangalore in India. It is as though we were being prepared for the tensions we would encounter in Africa.

The year was 1980. We flew from India to Nairobi, to find Kenya's North Eastern Province in an uproar that had mushroomed from an inci-

Thatched roofs of Somali huts near Garissa were deliberately torched when hostilities began.

dent in a bar at Garissa. Smouldering resentments burst into open flame after a group of armed bandits of ethnic Somali origin entered the bar and gunned down four policemen. Rumours later surfaced that they had been tracking and plotting specifically against one of these police officers who had earlier participated in the castration of a Somali. Whatever the reason or excuse, the results were far-reaching and long-lasting.

Ron Ward, one of the first CBM missionaries to serve in Kenya, met us at the Jomo Kenyatta airport and brought us up to date on happenings, including the burning of Somali huts in Garissa, with the loss of many lives. Huts in the *manyatta*, as that section of the city was called, differed from standard downtown housing. Rather than being square, of cement-block construction with corrugated metal roofs, *manyatta* residences were of a traditional style favouring circular walls of mud-plastered woven branches capped with a thatched roof. These burned like tinder. Furthermore, it was a simple matter to put a stick or a wire through the hasp on the outside of each door, with horrible and predictable results for those trapped inside.

North Eastern Province (NEP) was in turmoil as retaliatory acts of violence escalated between the bandits, known as *shifta*, and Kenyan authorities. In that environment there was considerable confusion, resulting in the hasty flight of a large number of civil servants and other civilians. It amounted to an exodus of non-Somali Kenyans, referred to as "down country people." The Somali, for the most part, are different in facial appearance from other Kenyans (the majority outside of NEP) whose languages belong to the Bantu group.

In this context Ron had a sobering proposal for us to consider when we stepped off the plane in Nairobi. With this fresh exodus still in full swing, he proposed that he take us to visit Garissa. Virginia and I agreed. Ron proceeded to Garissa the same day by bus. We were to follow later with his wife, Joan, after shopping in Nairobi for basic supplies not available in Garissa.

The importance of a trip to Nairobi's outdoor market to buy the ingredients for what Joan referred to as "Somali tea" was not evident to us at the time. After two or three mornings of this delicious, spicy beverage, which includes cardamom and ginger, I became a full supporter. Just after dawn one hears the sound of pestle and mortar hammering spices into powder. Then, in the cool of the morning, a steaming mug is delivered to the guest, and a fine new day begins under the clear sky that by late morning will become something of an inferno. For this is in Kenya's desert area.

The drive from Nairobi to Garissa began on paved roads of good quality as far as Thika, deteriorating from there with the passing of kilometres. From Mwingi, where one passes a control point, it became a desert track, acceptable in spots, worse in others, always abundant in dust. Sand, washboard and potholes abound. The conditions make this trip of seven or eight hours into something of an ordeal. For those who work in Garissa and beyond this travel is a routine of life. That particular day the tension began at Mwingi and continued through hour after hour of travel through uninhabited and inhospitable surroundings. Between Mwingi and Garissa

Several perilous adventures in northeastern Kenya involved this Land Rover.

we had two scares, but ended up being able to laugh at both. The return trip would be a different story.

Desert roads often create a mirage effect under the hot sun, blurring the shape of what one sees. I was at the wheel of the Land Cruiser when we rounded a corner to sight what appeared to be two sentries in the middle of the road. It was an improbable area for a checkpoint, without housing or town. I braked to a halt so we could assess the situation. The blob of each body was evident, and the profile of legs below, but still it didn't compute just right. Our conclusion was not immediate. In the end it looked okay to proceed and check out our theory. Sure enough, we had the precise rear view of two donkeys. We laughed, breathed deeply and drove on.

The second event was equally tense as we spotted a vehicle ahead stopped by the roadside with people standing around. We approached cautiously, for in this vast wilderness area the *shifta* would be entirely at home. This was their kind of terrain, where they could appear and disappear at will. Government vehicles had instituted an armed convoy system of travel, but we were travelling solitary. As we got closer Joan recognized acquaintances from Garissa hastily changing a tire. We exchanged information, and both we and they hurried on. Our arrival at Garissa was without incident.

The following day Ron took us on a courtesy call to the district officer at Garissa. Omar Sheik Farah is a wise and gracious gentleman in the true sense of that descriptive word. At that time there were not a lot of ethnic Somalis in high government office, so he was something of an exception. We were admitted to his office without delay, but it was some time before he was able to speak. He paced back and forth across his office, choking back tears, with never a word. He shook each hand, greeted us with gratitude then eventually addressed Ron.

"I don't know what kind of people you are. When my own Kenyan people are fleeing, you bring us guests." The welcome we received was very real. The bonds Ron was building with him were strong ones.

Life was simple on the compound that the Wards had arranged for themselves, their children and their Kenyan colleague Daniel Maina, and for other colleagues like ourselves who visited from time to time. It was known as the Garissa Community Centre, consisting of a series of rondeval huts, similar in appearance to Somali huts in the *manyatta*, but with adaptations. The centre had guest huts as well as separate sleeping huts for the Ward children, who visited periodically when school was not in session. The rondevals were all electrified, each had a cement floor and a sink. Waste water from the sink was piped out through the wall to disappear in the sand. Usually a banana tree or a bougainvillea plant was planted beside these unusual sources of water in the desert. The centre had a common kitchen where food was prepared for all, then carried to a larger hut of the same construction, centrally located. This larger rondeval doubled as both dining hall and meeting room. It had no chairs; everyone sat on mats. Some of us ate with our fingers, Somali style, though spoons and forks were available for those who preferred a more traditional approach. Chapatis, crepes and diced camel meat were favourites. Being granted the status of "elder," more or less, it was acceptable for me to locate where the centre pole served as my back rest.

Residences on the compound at Garissa adapted to the local building style.

Otherwise, a position along the outer wall was favoured. We left our shoes at the door.

Our several visits to the community centre at Garissa were always pleasant. Thatched huts are a very comfortable arrangement under the desert sun. Evening meals and talk sessions sometimes took place outside on mats in the comfortable evening air, moon or stars adding to the atmosphere. It was important always to check for scorpions. One starry night a scorpion ran across the hand of one of the Ward children, but there were no bites during our visits. Beyond the wire boundary that marked the perimeter of the compound there was a barren area, in fact one could argue that this barren area stretched off into infinity. Donkeys grazed these areas searching for a stray sprig of vegetation. Their braying on a moonlit night was one of the hallmarks of a visit to the community centre. Local belief had it that they were braying at the *jins*, the spirits.

Hostilities in NEP led to the first breakthrough in relationships between the community centre and the Somalis of the *manyatta*. The centre provided a number of services related primarily to health, nutrition, education, appropriate technology, agriculture, forestry and water. Programs were always developed as a direct result of consultations with the Somali community elders. Our visits were occasions for evaluating existing programs and examining the viability of programs that might be added. There had been regular interaction at the various service sites, but little breakthrough in terms of personal relationships. That changed with the outbreak of hostilities.

On the night of the first serious burning of the *manyatta* at Garissa, many Somalis were able to gather belongings and flee before either the torching parties or sparks carried by the wind reached their homes. To the surprise of those at the community centre, dozens of people came and unceremoniously dumped their bundles of personal possessions across the fence into the compound of the centre before fleeing into the night. This was the first sign that our personnel had established some considerable degree of trust and credibility with the people, who had tended to keep their distance.

Daniel Maina went through a time of personal testing, the results of which speak highly in his favour. At first he fled to his home region, north of Nairobi near the Aberdare Mountains where his Kikuyu people are concentrated. There he meditated for two or three days and sensed God's call to return to Garissa. Daniel swallowed his pride, apologized for having left, and resumed work with the Wards and others in Garissa. Daniel was teased unmercifully by Somalis: "Trouble comes, and you run off to your Kikuyu God in the hills." He did not give in to embarrassment, but persevered and helped to develop programs of significance to the community.

The community centre in Garissa had been established with the African Christian Church and Schools (ACC&S), an autonomous Kenyan denomination. The Wards, Bob and Anne Swann and others were the Canadian Baptist contribution. Daniel Maina and others represented the ACC&S. It was important to have that evident partnership.

In this time of civil unrest no outings or side trips away from Garissa were possible without permission. It was important that we make a trip to Dadaab. Getting travel permission required certain formalities, which included arranging for the obligatory armed guards. There were two, and they sat in the back with what I referred to as their "can openers" between their knees. These were assault rifles, pointed at the roof. If the trigger were depressed with the safety catch in "off" position, the result on the vehicle's roof would have been like that of a can-opener.

On that day's outing Ron Ward was at the wheel and I was in the passenger seat. Always interested in animals, I kept a keen eye on the countryside and often shot a finger out the window to point out a *gerinuk*, a grazing camel, or whatever appeared. I failed to notice the repeated "click" from the back, and Joan kept the secret to herself in amusement. With each pointing of my arm a nervous sentry would cock his rifle. They thought I was pointing out *shifta* bandits. Coming back into town we met a truck with its own sentry and with passengers in the back. We paused briefly for an exchange of greetings and news. The following morning we received a report that one of their passengers had been shot travelling through the area we had crossed earlier.

As we came to the end of that visit, our return to Nairobi had to be arranged for the day and hour that an official government convoy would be rolling. Otherwise we would not be allowed past the control barrier at the edge of Garissa, by the bridge. The danger provoking convoy travel lay in the gangs of *shifta* bandits that attacked vehicles from time to time, robbing and sometimes killing. The distinctive feature of the convoy was that it carried armed guards in the first vehicle (usually the bus, I believe) and again in the last vehicle. The inconveniences of the convoy lay in its agonizing snail's pace and in the clouds of dust kicked up by the vehicles ahead as it plodded across the scrub-on-sand that is the desert of North Eastern Province.

That day we loaded into the Land Cruiser, said our goodbyes at the Garissa Community Centre and made our way to the convoy's assembly point, just across the bridge. Passing the control barrier, Ron edged the vehicle slowly past an assortment of vehicles that had gathered.

"John, I don't think we should travel in the convoy today," he commented. I'm not sure I would have had the faith or the nerve to do that, if I'd been at the wheel. Nobody challenged us as we moved slowly past the bus and out onto the open track heading for Nairobi. We watched behind, there was no signal insisting that we stop, so in due time we picked up whatever speed was possible under the conditions and settled into the morning's drive across the desert.

Well into the trip there is one distinctive feature in what is otherwise a long stretch of sameness, sand and scrub bushes and thorn trees. That feature is an angular turn in the road. At about that point we met a column of men on foot, coming toward us on our left in single file. As they came nearer we saw that they carried animal skins rolled under their arms. When we heard the news on our arrival in Nairobi it became obvious that they carried automatic weapons in those skins. Ron did not change speed, swerve, brake or otherwise react. The narrowness of the track meant that we passed them at a distance of little more than an arm's length. With faces straight ahead, they neither greeted us nor acknowledged our presence in any way, not even by a glance. We had a good look at their faces. We passed safely and discussed who they might be. Would they be pastoralists caring for camels or goats? Not likely. The lack of animals, the numbers, the clothing, the marching style—nothing matched. They were not decked out in the standard costume of either Borana or Somali. They were a mystery.

That afternoon we crossed into what was considered the safe part of Kenya as we left North Eastern Province and passed through the control barrier at Mwingi. From there the roads progressively improved, and in the late afternoon we arrived at Nairobi, where Ron made his habitual phone contact with Joan back in Garissa to announce our safe arrival. He was greeted by an anxious voice and then a flood of praise to God that we were unharmed.

"The helicopters have been bringing in the dead and the wounded from the convoy. It was attacked at the big bend in the road. The count seems to be twelve dead and eighteen wounded. Praise God that you're safe."

What is safety, and how does one define it? A quiet street in Burlington, Ontario seemed a safe place for our family in 1978, yet there our son John fell fifteen metres from a tree and suffered serious brain injury. Angola and Kenya seemed like highly perilous situations, as did Yugoslavia, Croatia, Bosnia and Zaire. Safety is a relative term, and we have come to see it as being linked with pursuing the purposes of God.

The greatest value does not lie in the greatest number of days lived, but rather in how those days are lived, for whom, and for what purpose. On the day God sees fit to take one or another of us to himself he is no less faithful than on the day he chooses to protect us from what is apparent harm, and to give us additional days of existence on this planet.

In a similar vein, what is adventure? The era of television has heightened a search for the dramatic, often in terms of physical danger, especially violence. *Webster's New Collegiate Dictionary* cites as its first definition of adventure: "an undertaking involving danger and unknown risks." In reality, life itself is an adventure, yet the word implies a more deliberate undertaking in which one is not deterred by the risks. In that sense I look back over our years spent in cross-cultural mission for our Lord as the ultimate in adventure. Many highlights emerge, beginning with languages and cultures that are at first unknown, then eventually become a natural part of one's daily experience. There is the rich drama of lives that have taken on new meaning, cultures that have taken on new richness, communities that have been revitalized. These are the rewards of that adventure.

At the end of the 1970s, when Canadian Baptists and the African Christian Church and Schools came to the end of a ten-year partnership in the home territory of the ACC&S, they resolved together to take on a new adventure in service of our Lord. That resolve led to the opening of the work in North Eastern Province around which this chapter has been written.

Earlier, to research some facets of programs that might eventually be developed, we had chartered a small plane and visited a number of points in north and northeast Kenya. It was a joint CBM and ACC&S undertaking. Just before noon one day our delegation arrived at Mandera, a fron-

With Bishop Nathan Ngala of the Africa Brotherhood Church, at Machakos, Kenya.

tier town from which one can look north into Ethiopia and East into Somalia. We were to lunch as guests of the district officer at his rustic residence, established in what had been the old frontier fort of colonial times. This had been constructed from logs and earth, to resist cannon fire, with massive walls that made it delightfully cool even in the heat of the desert.

We had an hour or so free before the noon meal. Pastor Samuel Mugo had heard that prices were attractive at a market across the border in Somalia. Would it be possible for him to go over there to see if he could locate a pair of shoes to take back as a gift to his wife? The district officer made his driver and jeep available to Pastor Mugo and our other travelling companion, Stephen Nganga. They invited me to go along. Normally, immigration officers on the Somali side of the frontier would have spotted me and prevented my entering Somalia, where, unknown to me, the Soviet Union had established a missile site with missiles trained on Nairobi. I was blissfully unaware of any political overtones. Normal process went by the board as we crossed the frontier that day. Because the Somali officials knew the jeep of the D.O. they simply waved us through. It was a closed vehicle and my white skin was not visible. We passed a half hour or more there in the market. Samuel purchased the shoes—bright yellow ones. We chatted with a number of people and even took a few pictures. Re-entering Kenya we were again waved back through the post.

At the luncheon table the topic of brother Mugo's shopping expedition came up. Yes, he had found a pair of shoes. When the D.O. heard that there was a Canadian presence in the expedition he froze as if struck dead. I cannot say that he turned white—he was a native son of Kenya—but all the emotional components that we associate with that expression swept over him as he realized the implications. Had we been discovered by police, military or immigration people, imprisonment was not a possibility; it would have been a certainty. A western visitor found in that area a month earlier was still in prison. The gravity of our case would have been compounded by two factors—we were not officially stamped into Somalia, and we were carrying cameras. This had indeed been an undertaking involving danger and unknown risks, and it was done in total innocence—all for a pair of yellow shoes.

The many visits to Kenya included weeks spent in visits, consultations and interaction with the Africa Brotherhood Church. The experiences were far less dramatic than those shared above, but they were profoundly fulfilling—and demonstrate the grace of God no less than the more sensational episodes.

9
Indonesia
Overbearing North Americans

Early in February of 1971 my flight from Singapore was making its final approach to a landing in Jakarta, Indonesia. This was the first contact that any staff of Canadian Baptist Ministries had made with Indonesia, and I was investigating it as a field of potential involvement.

I watched the view ahead of the wing, eager to register those first impressions. As my plane circled over the city, coming lower and lower in its approach to the runway, I was impressed with the amount of water, virtually everywhere. So much irrigation, I thought to myself. As we came really low I saw that what I had taken for irrigation was halfway up to the windows of many of the houses in the poorer section of town. On the ride from the airport into the city I concluded that Indonesians were accustomed to dealing with crises such as flooding with considerable calm. A man was sitting on a chair in front of his house, reading a newspaper. Water was lapping around the seat of his chair, yet he himself remained dry and apparently unperturbed, his feet propped up on another chair.

The first day and night in Jakarta were facilitated by Ed Sanders, a Southern Baptist missionary who set me up with a translator, Anton, who would also accompany me as guide on a further internal flight to Manado, in North Sulawesi. I was to find out that he translated; he did not interpret and he did not provide any commentary. Perhaps I didn't know enough to ask for his guidance in the right way. His English was adequate but he was not sufficiently confident of himself or his assignment to offer any guidance. Neither Anton nor anyone else informed me that the polite church leaders who hosted my visit to North Sulawesi were uncomfortable with the conditions under which Canadian Baptists were now beginning to work in our new task force arrangement that would soon be implemented on three continents. This was to be a new style of working for Canadian Baptists, and something of a departure from the way other mission organizations were working. In short, it was to be a partnership in which CBM would provide people but no program money, and for a defined period of time, then to be withdrawn.

The smiles and friendly warmth of the people gave me no clues that I was propounding policies they found difficult to accept. Behind these smiling faces and the amiable dispositions of remarkable people who also provided such marvellous hospitality there were very serious reservations as to policy. I took the gently worded questions as a search for information rather than questions expressing reservations. Returning to Toronto, my report indicated that the leaders of this young denomination appeared to be in agreement with the conditions, which I had certainly outlined in adequate detail.

For a man with anthropological background, the errors I made on my first visit to Indonesia in early 1971 were laughable—only because in the long run they appear not to have become tragic. In all this I look back and see the grace of God abundantly at work, minimizing my shortcomings. It was in September 1970 that I took office as general secretary of what was then the Canadian Baptist Overseas Mission Board (CBOMB). September and October had been crammed full with all manner of orientation which focused particularly on India and Bolivia. We spent much less time on Angola and Congo, because I had lived and worked there. There were brief sessions on Kenya, which was shaping up to be our organization's next area of engagement. Bob Berry and I were coming on as new staff people, and Dr. Orville Daniel, the retiring general secretary, conducted a series of intensive orientation sessions for us. There was no orientation on Indonesia, since nobody from our mission had ever been there.

Dyak housing along the Kapuas River in West Kalimantan, Indonesia, built on stilts.

A few years later, five minutes of cultural explanation by the Byrne and Card families, who, in that time, had become our pioneer missionaries to Indonesia, were sufficient to unlock the mysteries of communicating with Indonesians. Listeners affirm a speaker by periodic lifting of the eyebrows—nothing verbal required. When the eyebrows are not raised, and the listener continues looking the speaker in the eye with steady, unwavering attention, the listener is expressing disagreement—nothing verbal required. One could say that in their own refined, cultural way these people were in fact screaming their disagreement to the conditions I had described. Confrontation was not their style. If I posed a direct question about acceptance, and even produced documents for mutual signatures, those features of our interaction were accepted as part of the overbearing style for which North Americans were known. Nor did anyone inform them that this visitor from Canada was totally unaware of their difficulty in accepting the conditions outlined. There was nobody who could stand between us to express to them my deep longing for genuine understanding, and my desire to reach consensus.

We have often seen the grace of God come into play to cover our weaknesses, our ignorance and our failings as well as our more blatant transgressions. No deliberate deception was involved by either party, and God seems to take into consideration the intentions of the heart. These initial misunderstandings never became insurmountable, even though they made life and ministry more difficult for the families who became the Canadian Baptist pioneers living and working in the Indonesian society.

Other features of my initial report led the Byrne and Card families to wonder whether John Keith was somehow out of touch with reality on that first visit. My report spoke of the peaceful tranquility of life in an Indonesia village. The quiet was totally a feature of where I was housed, of the buffer zone that had been created around this first special visit of a Canadian. I had been sheltered from barking dogs, screaming children at play, and the myriad sounds that make up normal daily life in an Indonesian village.

To emphasize how easy it is to get a wrong picture during a short visit, consider my report on the food. I described it as mild, tasty and delightful, just as I like it. That is how I remembered the food when I was writing my reports, but there was more to that conclusion than meets the eye. My memories focused on the overall experience, and not necessarily what had been laid out on the groaning tables of the first *pesta* spread before me. This feast, like others to follow, was spread out with incredible variety on long tables in what we would call buffet style.

What I did not recollect is that in my exploratory samplings I gravitated toward the lightly spiced foods, and when I went back for seconds it would definitely have been for the foods that pleased my palate most. These tastes were diligently noted, obviously discussed by all, and carefully recorded. There followed a series of these bountifully supplied collective meals. They featured great variety and profusion, but always along the theme of my preferred style, and only mildly seasoned. All this without a word of comment. My habitual seconds (perhaps even thirds) of one special dessert made from immature coconut even led it to be renamed locally as "John's pie."

The strong personal faith of Pastor Alex Tairas extended to all facets of life.

The memory banks of the cooks proved infallible in later years. Those favourites would always appear, but now along with the spicier foods enjoyed by their own new Canadian families Byrne and Card. Becoming accustomed to our tastes and our dislikes, one of the Indonesian hosts or hostesses would invariably sidle up to me and mention that I need not sample certain dishes with darker meat; they had learned that I had no special appreciation for meat of the dog or the field rat.

Reflecting on Indonesia, it is not food that comes to mind, or those cultural misunderstandings of the first visit. Outstanding were the remarkable church leaders in this Minahasa area of Northern Sulawesi. They spearheaded the growth of this young denomination, which began around the end of World War II. About three families were prominent in leadership at the outset, but we came to learn that there were many others as well.

Alex Tairas, known as *Pendeta* Alex, (*pendeta* meaning pastor or teacher), was one of those leaders. Sometime during the 1980s, Alex and

"Opa" Williams conducted his river ministries from this houseboat.

I, with Malcolm Card, needed to visit Pontianak in West Kalimantan, where the denomination was developing a missionary outreach. Canadian Baptists were to become part of that outreach, and our visit of investigation was preparing the foundations. We faced a complication. Virginia, who was travelling with me on that visit, was not at all well. We left her in Jakarta and undertook this visit of about four days to Pontianak. A return reservation was not available, but we would work that out in Pontianak on arrival, or so we thought.

At the airline office in Pontianak we were given the distressing information that all flights back to Jakarta were full until a week from next Tuesday—unless, of course, the airstrip was dry. The runway was short, and this was rainy season. On days when the runway was dry a few extra passengers could be added, and under those circumstances I would have a place. *Pendeta* Alex's response was an immediate smile.

"Then we have no problem. We'll just pray that it does not rain."

Longhouses among the Karo Batak of Sumatra have a distinctive profile.

The buildup of thunder heads in Indonesia can be impressive, as it was on the day I was to return to Jakarta. The departure time was late morning. *Pendeta* Alex caught me slipping outside to look at that buildup of clouds in the west. Very seriously he said, "Do not look up in that direction. We have given the problem to God." I tried to honour his advice, but peripheral vision made me very aware of the imposing black wall that hung there in threatening fashion during our drive to the airport, and through the time awaiting the departure call for my flight. No rain fell. As my flight was announced (Alex and Malcolm were to remain for a few days) Alex accompanied me to the gate. He looked up and pointed with a broad smile to the ominous cloud bank, which had not advanced as one might have expected. His farewell was a single phrase. "Jesus Christ, the same yesterday, today and forever."

The rest of the story came later in a message from Malcolm Card: immediately after the plane's departure there was a torrential downpour such as he had seldom or never seen.

Pastor Dicky Pelandang was a fellow seminary teacher with CBM families Byrne and Card.

During our twenty years of interaction with Indonesia Virginia and I also had a chance to look at the option of becoming partners with these remarkable Indonesians in their outreach to another of Indonesia's major islands, Sumatra. On that trip we accompanied Canadian pastor Jack Longhurst and Indonesian pastor Ronny Welong.

The traditional Karo Batak residential pattern was the longhouse, and we had an opportunity to see how the many families lived under one roof without the dividers that our own society would consider essential for privacy. We noted how they solved problems such as open cooking fires inside, on a raised wooden floor, under a thatched roof. Without skill and proper attention that arrangement would spell disaster. The solutions they had devised included a fire pit, complete with stones, in something like a raised sandbox.

We visitors were hosted in a private home. It had a kitchen innovation that I have not seen duplicated anywhere else in the world. As in other areas of Indonesia, the living space was one flight of stairs up from the ground. Farm implements were stored at ground level, under the living space. Beside the sink in the kitchen upstairs, a hole in the working surface of the counter led to a wooden chute. Where that chute led was a mystery until one went downstairs and around the outside of the house to the privy. There, parked across the path day and night was a huge sow who seemed to have learned to sleep on her feet, her mouth open precisely in line with a slight outward turn of the chute. She didn't need to be penned, her site was too productive to abandon. Whatever was deposited from above—water, vegetable peels, table scraps, it was all mainlined to the waiting mouth of Mrs. Sow.

In this private home our sleeping quarters were in a double bed behind a curtain in the corner of the room that served as sitting room, dining room and kitchen. We were excused to retire well before midnight, while a number of visitors from the community continued their conversations outside the curtain. A charming little lad of three or so would toddle over occasionally and peer through the curtains to make sure we were okay. Eventually he, his parents and the others took their farewell, but a messenger soon arrived to inform us that we were invited to come to the

One noted a radiance and vitality among Indonesian colleagues.

longhouse to preach. Immediately. Those travelling with us seemed to think that this was an invitation not to be turned down. We dressed hastily and went to the long house, where we were guests of one of the eight resident families, the other seven families listening in. My message was in English, translated to Indonesian, then translated again to Karo Batak. I can't recall what message I might have delivered at that time of night, but I remember sitting cross-legged on the woven mat, my Bible in front of me in the dim light of a kerosene lamp. One learns to travel prepared for all such eventualities.

Our sleeping arrangements on the following night were also unforgettable. Virginia and I had learned to travel with two single-size mosquito nets in our luggage, facilitating sleep even when mosquitoes were heavy. Jack Longhurst was given a single cot, we a double bed, in a large open space over a store. The shop owner and her family were sleeping

Dyak seminary students in West Kalimantan, formerly Borneo.

behind temporarily erected sheets of plywood, nearby. Considerate of Jack's need to sleep as well, we set up supporting cords for the mosquito nets in a way that would hold one of our nets over Jack's bed, the second net crosswise over the head and shoulders portion of our bed, our feet covered by a sheet.

I slept soundly, missing out on an instalment of late-night action. Virginia felt some small animal roaming around on the sheet stretched over her feet. It was a rat. Next she heard the noise and felt the impact as a cat pounced on the rat. Considerately, the cat removed the rat to the floor to complete the kill and enjoy her lunch. Virginia heard the crunching of bones. At earliest light I was awakened with the timid request to see what might be on the floor by the foot of the bed. The rat's tail was there as evidence, but little else. Following the crunchy lunch the cat jumped up on the bed again and curled up near Virginia's feet. Not so accustomed to pets, Virginia insists that she spent the rest of the night with her knees curled up under her chin. But she didn't reject that second visit of her protector.

Janet Clark shares tea and cakes with colleague Vera Tumundo in the Clark home at Karangan.

The first phase of CBM involvement in Indonesia took us to work on the Minahasa tip of North Sulawesi. Phase two was on Kalimantan, formerly Borneo, which is a much larger land mass in a setting of tropical rain forest. For centuries its rivers were the highway to and from the interior, an area where deforestation is the by-product of the world market's hunger for mahogany. The logging industry is a big part of the local economy, with its rafts of lumber that are floated down to Pontianak either for the sawmills or for direct export as logs. Debris from this use of the waterway adds to the danger of breaking propeller shear-pins when travelling on the river. In our case it meant hours moored to branches overhanging the bank of this river running through tropical rain forest, before hailing people of goodwill who towed us to a proper mooring where repairs could be made the next day.

There is no denying that for those who have grown up in Canada's climate the tropical rain forest holds an irresistible fascination, whether by day or by night. By day the lush greens, the bright colours and the shades of light and darkness scream the richness of warmth, moisture and sunlight. By evening it is the sounds, and the range of the imagination that drifts in harmony with those sounds, that are memorable. These are enjoyable byproducts of the endless travel that, on the other hand, deprives one of a settled existence and of being with family.

10
Brazil
Natural born optimists

A great many Brazilians seem to face life and the world with a certain light-hearted optimism that gives them a more cheery outlook on life than many other nationalities. During the two decades when my visits to Brazil were frequent there was something of a national ethos that depicted their land as a country of the future, upward bound and unstoppable. I recollect two phrases that seemed to appear with regularity and which reflected this outlook. *Tudo azul* (literally, "everything blue") carried the same connotation as our "all is rosy." *Deus é Brasileiro* went even further, affirming that God is a Brazilian. More correctly, God is a male Brazilian.

Brazilians do indeed have a lot going in their favour. Theirs is a vast country with rich resources in population, agricultural land and mineral resources, and with a wide variety of climatic conditions ranging from tropical to temperate zones. The Brazilian population is heavily weighted toward youth, and they consider the future to be on their side. We found in the Baptist churches an ease in accepting the attitude that with God all things are possible.

Brazilians think of themselves as winners, whether in soccer, or in life itself. Their attitude of confidence is often reflected in *piadas*, the stories they tell of themselves. One of the themes in these recurring stories involves beating Texans at their own game of bragging.

It seems that a Texan visiting Rio de Janeiro was emphasizing to his cab driver just how big things were in Texas. The taxi driver kept countering with comments on the speed with which Brazil was developing. The cabby deliberately detoured to drive past the Maracaná football stadium, the largest in the world at the time, but deliberately made no comment about it.

"What is that building?" the Texan asked, to which the cabby replied, "I don't know, it wasn't there this morning."

My familiarity with the Portuguese language gave ready access to Brazil and its people. My Lisbon accent was considered quaint, and unusual for a North American, but was graciously tolerated. I have always been conscious of that difference in accent that makes my speech amusing to listeners, even though I may be understood. For me, at least, that awareness of being quietly laughed at tends to erode my confidence and to reduce effectiveness. This experience leads me to encourage young people beginning international careers to do their language study in a socio-linguistic context that is compatible with the area where they will be serving.

My first working visit to Rio de Janeiro was set up to undertake discussions with church leadership about assisting them in their work. It was perhaps a weakness of my relational style that when I arrived in a country I wanted to get straight to work. That is not necessarily a positive trait when building relationships across cultures. The program, as I tried to set it up, normally began with a scheduled meeting with denominational office holders, specifically to outline the thinking and philosophy of my sponsoring body (CBM), and to share the guidelines I had been given, within which we could strike working agreements. From there we would proceed to more specific negotiations about what was needed, and whether CBM might be able to participate in reaching the established goals.

Prior to 1975 CBM and its personnel had no ministry contacts in Brazil. Arriving at Rio de Janeiro, I had planned to start off with my usual official consultation. Pastor João Falcão Sobrinho was my Brazilian counterpart and gracious host. He had a counter-proposal.

"Yes, we'll set up a meeting, but first there are things I want you to see so you can understand who we are and how we do God's work." He proceeded to set up a day's outing with Pastor Clovis Pereira, whose home mission assignment was in one of Rio's notorious slums, known as *favelas*. We spent the morning together, travelling in areas where no outsider would normally be safe. In fact, we were in areas where, at that time, Brazil's own police did not dare to venture, except in strength. Because of his

"Falcão", João Falcão Sobrinho, welcomed John Keith and Lynn Stairs to Brazil.

work there, Clovis was known, respected and loved; he and anyone with him could move around with the same freedom as those who lived there.

These *favelas* are like open sores on the face of the easily-eroded mountainside just behind the striking city. Rio has the waterfront at its front door; its panorama is punctuated by the famous Sugarloaf rock formation in the bay and the towering *Corcovado* mountain over its right shoulder, where a huge statue portrays a standing Christ with his arms stretched wide over the city. It has the slums at its back. These features combine to make Rio de Janeiro the distinctive and beautiful city that is so attractive to tourists. But the *favelas* are not pretty.

Many features have combined to create these slums. Migration to the city, poverty, crime, alcohol and gambling all are significant contributors to the subculture of the *favelas*. There on the hillside, on land often too steep for economical construction of valuable residences, the inhabitants have put together their hovels, using scraps of plastic sheeting, cardboard, pieces of metal or wood, and whatever else can be worked into a shelter against the elements.

As we proceeded into one *favela* Pastor Clovis gave me a surprising assignment.

"See if you can guess which of these places belong to members of our church."

How could I know that? Anyway, when I noted one that was more attractive, neater than the others, I tentatively suggested that maybe this one might be a candidate.

"Correct. You speak our language, check it out for yourself."

As we went closer the owners greeted the pastor warmly, then I heard directly from them how the reality of the presence of Jesus Christ in their lives had made a difference, a complete reversal of their former situation. As we proceeded deeper into the *favela* I was able to identify, by this guessing process, a number of Baptist families, then confirm the reality of my guess as we visited together briefly. I suspected that perhaps the church had made a direct contribution in money or materials toward the improvement on the housing. Not so.

"Our task is to introduce people to Jesus Christ. It is he who makes the difference in their lives, then the people change their environment."

With slight variations I heard the same story again and again. Lives had been changed. With them, priorities changed. Alcohol and gambling were left behind; the resources and energies formerly squandered were redirected toward family life and the improvement of living conditions. The changes didn't happen all at once but they were real, visible and verifiable.

When I later had my consultation with Pastor Falcão and other mission and church leaders it went well. By then I had been given a significant glimpse at who these Brazilian Baptists were and how they undertook their work. Factors having to do with language, migration, culture, national outlook and a number of other components all fed into an eventual working relationship between Canadian Baptist Ministries and the Brazilian Baptist Convention. This partnership serves as something of a model for the post-colonial style of mission relationship.

Perhaps the most notable evidences emerged in the mutual invitations from Canada and Brazil to receive assistance from each other's workers. In each instance the receiving country establishes the program goals. This arrangement is now more than twenty years old. CBM has been working toward that same maturity of relationship and interaction in all of its geographical areas of involvement for three decades and more. Economic, social and historical factors in Brazil definitely made the goal easier to achieve in that country than in many other areas. The Brazilians who have served as pastors in Canadian cities have made valuable contributions that went far beyond their work with Portuguese-speaking populations.

Lynn and Hannah Stairs, who had been our working colleagues in both Angola and the Congo, became the workers who pioneered for CBM in the state of Mato Grosso du Sul. In the early 1970s

Lynn and Hannah Stairs were CBM pioneers in working with Brazilian Baptists.

this was the wild west of Brazil, as bridges were built across the mighty Paraná river that had been the frontier of settlement. This push to the west opened up the rain forests to logging, land clearing and colonization. Trucks swarmed along the new highways, carrying families with all their belongings, pursuing their fortunes in a trek toward the expanding west. The name of the state began as a descriptive term, *Mato Grosso* meaning "thick jungle," for it had been just that before being opened to settlers.

There was little patience with anyone, especially foreigners, who raised the ecological questions posed by the destruction of rain forests, or who raised questions about the rights of indigenous populations who lived there. The treatment of native peoples by North Americans during our own westward expansion was considered to have removed our right to address parallel issues in Brazil.

There was a brief span of time, measured in decades at the most, when the western frontier of Brazil resembled the wild west of North America. It was not uncommon to see groups of men on horseback on dusty streets, some wearing side arms. "Justice" was often quick; shootings on the street were not unknown. But sophistication arrived fast; the streets were soon paved, and new cities burgeoned. Year by year the changes were striking. The push to open land for colonization, ranching and crop agriculture overrode any appeals for restraint or moderation based on depletion of ancient virgin rainforests, or to the global effect that would come as a result.

Following Lynn and Hannah Stairs a number of other families were soon appointed to Brazil. At the outset, the participation of CBM personnel in Brazilian Baptist programs was principally in the area of training leadership for the rapidly growing churches. At first they worked almost exclusively in institutions, as those were the tasks to which we were invited. But the logic that had put us in touch with Brazil initially was closely linked to long-standing commitments in Angola, which have been interrupted by approximately thirty-seven years of warfare. The concept was that workers could learn language, remain active in productive service, and be ready to enter Angola on short notice.

Because both Angola and Brazil use Portuguese in educational institutions, a number of ministry linkages between the two countries were possible. The Phillips and Janzen families, recruited initially for Angola, were assigned to Brazil "on hold," anticipating that political turmoil in Angola might subside enough for them to reside and work there. It did not work out that way. A number of promising student families from Angola were sponsored by CBM to pursue theological training in Brazilian seminaries. The first three of these, Buza, Cufo and Ganda, have since returned to Angola to continue their ministry. Two young Brazilian women who studied under Canadian Baptist teachers in Mato Grosso do Sul have had an extended and productive ministry in Angola. Karl Janzen and sometimes his wife Kathy, while still based in Brazil, made periodic extended excursions into Angola to conduct seminars and for general

Brazil's Pantanal. The Logos is tied up by the small house where Keiths encountered mosquitoes, piranha and a large constrictor that threatened to swallow a pig.

encouragement and assistance to the Angolan churches, which have been working in the face of many and serious obstacles.

Ministry assignments that began in the state of Southern Mato Grosso eventually expanded by invitation into the states of Tocantins, São Paulo, Pará, and to the national capital district, Brasilia, occasioning enchanting research visits to other tropical regions of the country to undertake investigation of tasks and invitations that for one reason and another Canadian Baptist Ministries was not able to pursue.

Mato Grosso do Sul's vast swampland known as the Pantanal feeds multiple watercourses emptying into the Paraguay River, flowing south through both Paraguay and Argentina to empty into the South Atlantic near Buenos Aires. Visits to the Pantanal have made a marked impression on me and on other Canadians, both volunteers and missionaries, who have participated there. Virginia and I visited the Pantanal in 1987.

Virginia displays her success in catching a piranha. Sleeping quarters were cramped considering the intense heat.

Land is not at a premium in the Pantanal. There are huge *fazendas,* where thousands of cattle graze. One rancher we visited along the way commented that he calculates on placing one cow per grazing hectare, and that the natural grass of the Pantanal is such a balanced food that he does not need to give his cattle any mineral supplement. Much of the grazing land lies so low and so close to the water level that surprise floods may drown thousands of cattle. The same rancher commented that crocodile hide hunters were disturbing the ecological balance. Crocodiles, he said, eat a lot of piranha. With the reduction of the crocodile population the piranha were becoming super abundant. We saw a few crocodiles, one of them enormous, but they were not in abundance.

Other wildlife on the Pantanal included varieties of waterfowl, and a particularly beautiful variety of kingfisher with a green back, a white neck-ring and a rufous breast. After all, I would take special note of the kingfisher, since we have named our home at Clear Lake *The Kingfish-*

er's Perch. (On Clear Lake I'm the kingfisher.) One of the noted animals of the Pantanal is the world's largest rodent, the *Capivara.* We saw a number of them, and ate its flesh more than once, rather a delicacy. It stands less than a meter in height and has a large rodent's head that is not particularly attractive. Because its food consists of marshland roots and tubers, its meat is safe for human consumption.

Don Fraser, left, chats with the Pantanal project's first boat captain, José Valamatos.

The Pantanal looks particularly glamorous in nature videos, which permit the viewer to bypass the three factors which make life so uncomfortable there—heat, humidity and mosquitoes. Riverboat ministries have been designed to bring hope and help to the sparse human population strung out along these watercourses. They are people who are isolated and who, for the most part, have not had access to health care or education. The riverboat ministries undertaken with Brazilian Baptists bring them both physical and spiritual input, and have changed their quality of life.

Pastor José Valamatos and his wife Eunice were our hosts as we set out on the *Logos One,* which José had welded together himself, not having been able to purchase a suitable existing boat on the river at that time. Their three children accompanied us as we first drove sixty kilometres from the Valamatos' home base at Corumbá and then boarded this little vessel docked at Murinho, where the road from Corumbá to Campo Grande crosses the Paraguay River. From there we chugged along down river to Porto Esperança and tied up at the bank of the lagoon where a modest house served as their ministry base away from home.

Laurence and Kathy Cheveldayoff (affectionately known as Chevy I and Chevy II) have spearheaded more recent facets of riverboat ministry in the Pantanal. The conditions I describe here apply equally to their situation.

My ledger for February 1987 fails to record the actual temperature we experienced but notes that in the previous year the thermometer at Corumbá went up to fifty-two degrees Celsius, equivalent to one hundred and twenty-five degrees Farenheit. We heard considerable commentary on the seemingly endless eight days and nights when the temperature had failed to drop below forty-three degrees Celsius (about one hundred and eight Farenheit).

The heat and the humidity reinforce each other. Along the channels of this swampy vastness it is the excessive humidity that makes these elevated temperatures so oppressive. It was unrealistic to expect that one could live and work in dry clothing, even with constant changes, yet clothing was important as a protection against both sun and mosquitoes. Someone living in the city might find periods of relief by installing air conditioning, but the work in Brazil was not run under that kind of budget. Out on the little *Logos* one did not even consider that as an option. In any event, such a luxury would create insurmountable obstacles to any developing relationship with the population, who have to live with these conditions year in and year out. The water, with its various hazards, was there for bathing.

The mosquitoes can be described, but are really understood only through experience. Captain Valamatos referred to "learning to inhale mosquitoes." It was hazardous to breathe with one's mouth open, especially in the evening. At one juncture I paused and indulged in the diversion of estimating (for the record) that there were about three hundred mosquito bites on my swollen right ankle. José commented that the contribution of mosquitoes to society seems to be that they are busy lowering the blood pressure of the population.

The following notes are from my ledger entry for February 27, 1987:

- Visited family living in a cavernous warehouse at Porto Esperança.

- No sign of beds anywhere (nor any mosquito nets). Hordes of mosquitoes.

- All members of the family illiterate. They salt a few fish.

- We used grass switches to reduce the number of mosquitoes, but even then they swarmed under our glasses.

That evening, bathing in the lagoon, warm as its waters might be, provided a relatively cool comfort. Virginia chose to shower in the little house on the shore, conscious of the abundance of piranha in the lagoon. I joined the men in their swim, assured that those carnivorous fish normally go into a feeding frenzy only when there is a taste of blood in the water. It was all right to bathe. A neighbour did warn José's teenage son Daniel to stay away from the spot a few metres down river where some people were cleaning fish. While we were bathing someone pointed out a crocodile making his way along the edge of the reeds at the other side of the lagoon. Perhaps the most disconcerting part of that evening's refreshing swim was the presence of harmless little fish that kept nudging my back. They seemed to nip, though they did not break the skin, and they were definitely not piranha.

The following morning's adventure interrupted us while we were ashore and having coffee at the breakfast table. The woman, who lived alone on the next property, was shouting.

"This snake is going to swallow my pig."

We all ran over to where a relatively small pen with a wooden floor and railings had been built on three or four logs to keep it up off the ground. Her hens had alerted her to the danger. The huge constrictor (which they identified as *sucuri*) had taken refuge under the floor between two of the logs. As usual, Pastor Valamatos was not short on plans.

"Daniel, bring the harpoon and the gun."

"Now John, I'm going to harpoon it as close to the head as possible. When I pull it out, you shoot it through the head."

We did just that. The constrictor measured just over four meters, and its weight was estimated at nearly seventy-five kilograms, or about one hundred and fifty pounds. It certainly had the capacity to swallow the sow, and would probably have done so if not interrupted. It was promptly skinned and the skin was stretched to dry in the sun. Daniel enjoyed watching the piranha devour the carcass; they made short order of it. We were told that the piranha can strip the hide and all the flesh from a cow in a matter of minutes.

Let nobody reading this account think that I had pity for myself, being there on such a very brief interlude. Every experience of that visit enhanced my admiration and esteem for people of whatever nationality, whether Canadian or Brazilian, who make deliberate choices to live and work under these conditions to serve the needs of others in the name of Jesus. It is in honour of their services that I record these notes. Clearly it is the grace of God that permits his choice people to opt deliberately to minister under such conditions, and having begun, to persevere in such an environment.

Not all our adventures were dangerous ones. On one occasion Don and Ruth Fraser, just recently on board as Latin America representatives for CBM, were travelling with Virginia and me. We travelled by air shuttle from São Paulo to Rio, not bothering to make hotel reservations. We didn't need them. I knew an older hotel, pie-shaped, along the boulevard, and we would go there. It was reasonable in price, and space had never been a problem.

We collected our luggage, hailed a taxi and gave the driver our destination, only to find that it was boarded up and surrounded with scaffolding; it was under renovation. The taxi driver took us to the Trocadeiro, the Lancaster and a couple of others in Copacabana, but they were all full. The driver knew a friend who ran a hotel on Governor's Island that would be within our price range. He took us there, and the price was not the problem.

When Don and I tried to check in for one night the desk clerk was clearly uncomfortable, and ended up affirming that he had no room. That didn't seem to fit, since the keys all seemed to be hanging there in their cubbyholes behind his desk. His problem was that he was not used to customers with baggage—people who wanted to stay so long. Furthermore, the area was isolated, and they didn't serve meals or breakfast. Our taxi driver had his reputation to defend; he had brought us here. He persuaded the desk clerk to register us. None of us had ever seen hotel rooms with so many mirrors, even on the ceiling! We flew on the next day to our appointment in Marabá. If you're planning a visit to Rio, remember that neither the Frasers nor the Keiths recommend the Sunshine Hotel on Governor's Island.

On another trip to Brazil, this time coming from Kenya, the most direct passage was via South Africa. I needed to pause there long enough to write the Kenya reports while they were still fresh in my mind. During the early 1980s Virginia and I were regularly away from home for six months out of a year, on working assignments that took us from continent to continent. Travel agents would have booked us into accommodations too costly for our budget, so in places where we had no acquaintances we tended to make our own arrangements when possible. On an earlier trip through Johannesburg I had made notes on various hotels that we had scouted out, so for this particular stopover I had phoned in my reservation directly from our home to this little hotel in Jo'burg, and had given its address as a mail drop to our children and to the CBM office.

When I phoned I should have noted the amazement in the tone of the desk clerk who answered. But yes, he did confirm our reservation. We arrived to find that I had made a horrible mistake, and had chosen the wrong hotel from my notes. Having given its address as our mail drop we were committed to that hotel. We were to be there for about four nights. We checked in.

The lobby was dark and dismal, and in our earlier research tour we had not even given it consideration, but I got my notes wrong. Just how wrong did not become evident until the end of the first day, when we came down to find where we should have our evening meal. The lobby and the bar just beside it were thronged with men in lipstick, high heels, ear and nose rings, leather skirts, green hair, and other patterns of attire that do not fit our style. Little wonder the desk clerk had paused when Dr. and Mrs. John Keith from Lakefield, Ontario had phoned through their reservation to his hotel.

We made the best of it. For the remaining days there Virginia and I went out at noon for our main meal, then picked up juice and other simple items for an evening snack in our room. The reports got written and despatched; we received our mail; and in the evenings we didn't disrupt the men in the bar downstairs.

11
Russia and Ukraine
Glasnost and a hunger for the gospel

Even during the harshest years of the cold war, strong fraternal links were maintained between the Baptist World Alliance in Washington and the community of Baptist believers in the U.S.S.R. and other Eastern European countries. Baptists there also had connections with Western Europe as well as with the Canadian Baptist Federation. Baptists in Ontario and Western Canada worship in many of the languages of Eastern Europe. Outside communication with Eastern Europe was severely restricted prior to the era of *glasnost*. But the intense interest that accompanied prayers for those under the restrictive Communist regime kept opening corridors of communication which, although small, were nevertheless significant. In 1988 there was something of a breakthrough as denominational leaders Bob Berry, Dick Coffin, Bob MacQuade and Doug Moffatt, assisted and accompanied by Alex Piatocha, undertook a significant tour, first to the U.S.S.R. and then to China.

As *glasnost* began to offer at least a glimmer of hope for change, a Baptist family from Western Canada began testing the possibilities for more direct contact. Rev. Alex Piatocha and his wife Mary were both born in Ukraine. In the last week of July 1986 Alex approached CBM with an appeal for $5,000 to assist with a shipment of Bibles to Russia and Ukraine. It was the beginning of serious CBM interaction with Alex and Mary in ministry; this contact indirectly would lead us, the Keiths, to

Alex Piatocha introduces the Children's Bible to a congregation in Ukraine.

the Eastern European assignment that became the highlight of our career.

CBM colleagues were on summer vacation when Alex first approached us, so it fell to me to hear the Piatochas' remarkable story and to make the contacts that would help them with shipping costs. Alex, who had also served as chaplain to the Edmonton Eskimos football team, was pastoring in Alberta; Mary was employed with a grocery chain. As their contacts with Ukraine opened up they privately undertook a bold personal venture in ministry, and committed their own finances to it unreservedly.

The Piatochas secured a significant stock of Russian and Ukrainian Bibles, packed them in forty suitcases and took them as accompanied luggage on a visit to what was then the U.S.S.R. Their own roots reached back to an area of Ukraine west of Lutzk, toward the Polish border. Whatever assistance they may have had, they still depleted their personal resources to the point where Mary even cashed in her pension plan and invested the funds to help pay for these Bibles, suitcases, their tickets and the cost of excess baggage, which must have been considerable.

The story of their encounter with customs officials is captivating. Alex describes how Mary, while he himself was still discussing the contents of his suitcases with the official, was pulling the heavy suitcases one by one past the checkpoint.

"She could have been shot," he said. It was certainly a critical moment and a perilous procedure, given the harshness of the Soviet Union in those days. Mary has that kind of faith. It is the kind of faith that sees action accompanying prayer. They both acted boldly and by the grace of God that boldness became the instrument to open significant new doors. The relative ease with which such a project could be undertaken today must not detract from the remarkable feat of their having dared to do it in the 1980s.

During that early trip they established a link with a certain official who gave them his verbal clearance to bring in another shipment of Bibles Alex had been able to secure. Having used all of their personal and church-related resources, Alex came to CBM for assistance in paying shipping costs. It was this interaction that first alerted us to the changing situation in the Soviet Union. From that contact came Alex's invitation for Virginia and me to accompany them on a group visit in September 1989, and to be the special speakers at a conference for regional pastors and their wives at Kiev, in Ukraine.

Virginia and I were latecomers to Europe, but we came to realize, as the environment in Eastern Europe continued to open, that we had arrived at a significant time. In August of 1989 we flew via Helsinki to Moscow's Sheremetyevo airport. Our guides for the visit were Alex and Mary Piatocha. Their own main focus was on Ukraine, but entrance to the Soviet Union at that time was through Moscow. We proceeded to Kiev and other parts of Ukraine. Our integration into this working group of Canadians who spoke Ukrainian and who had family ties with the population, permitted us intimate and accurate insights into the little things that an outsider would not otherwise know how to interpret.

This was during the period of *glasnost* under Mikhail Gorbachev, a time when new events seemed to be breaking day by day. On our first weekend we were still in Moscow and I was invited to preach at the Baptist Church, one of the very few Protestant churches that had been allowed to function—albeit under very restrictive conditions—throughout the era of Stalin and his successors.

When we arrived at the church we noticed how obscure were its location and its markings. The church is situated on a side street; this was a government requirement. A street corner location for any place of worship was not an option. They were not permitted external symbols indicating it to be a church, and certainly they had no prominent sign. It turned out that on this particular Sunday morning I was to be the fourth and main speaker. I chose a text from John's Gospel, chapter eight, verses twelve to eighteen, and developed the theme "No darkness, no confusion, never alone." The church had seating for eight hundred people with another eight hundred standing. Pastor Vasili Logvinenko presided over the service, which ran for precisely two hours. I had a very definite sense that in this place and on this day I was not the main event. The presence of God was the main event.

Following the service we had an opportunity to share a meal with Pastor Logvinenko, who did not for a moment pretend to take credit for the unusual developments in his congregation at that time. He shared a few, and I record here one incident from my notes on that day.

One of his parishioners, a woman of humble standing, dreamed that there was a certain phone number she should call, but she had not dreamed what the topic of conversation should be. Unsure of what she should do about the dream, she consulted a fellow worshipper. That lady advised her to make the call and to offer the gift of a Bible, if the person who answered was open to receive it. The woman who answered the phone accepted gladly. Her comment was, "I have just buried my husband, and I didn't know where to turn."

The years and experiences that have passed have not diminished my admiration for God's servant Vasili Logvinenko, who had endured many hardships associated with leading this congregation during the difficult years of stringent control over Christian worship. His was virtually the only Protestant church in all of the Soviet Union that maintained continuous ministry throughout the Communist era. During one of my visits to Russia in the 1990s some of the younger people provided helpful insights on how Pastor Logvinenko had functioned.

These young people commented that many people in Christian leadership positions in various Eastern European countries were considered to have compromised their faith in order to keep the doors open in the churches they were serving. Not so Pastor Logvinenko.

"He never openly opposed a government decree. When instructed by government agents to shut down a program, he would shut it down. Then, within a few weeks, he would have developed something just different enough to survive for a time, until confronted again. He did not compromise, he was just wise."

The most lasting impression of that morning's worship service was the deep, dark beauty of its music, predominantly in a minor key. Somehow it expressed the emotion of their deep reverence for our all-powerful God, while giving voice to the pain growing out of two or more generations of believers' faithfulness unto death. Their tradition was one that refused to bow the knee to a secular power that declared their God to be irrelevant, in fact non-existent.

We encountered little or no resentment of the Communist era. It was interpreted as an instrument of God to purify and strengthen his church, and even to create the conditions under which awareness of God's love and redemption could expand. We were told, "The gospel was needed in Siberia. Our grandmothers, in chains, carried it there. They were often knocked to their knees in the snow, on that long hard march on foot to Siberia. They would get up again, dripping blood, and proceed on their way, in chains, singing hymns." A component of the majesty of that kind of dedication to Christ has permeated music and worship in Russia and the other states of the former Soviet Union.

Having experienced the depth and quality of church music in their homeland, we were able to understand a degree of the reaction of some Eastern Europeans to contemporary worship music used at heavily attended public worship services at Lillehammer, Norway, in July of 1994. The occasion was a massive assembly of the European Baptist Federation. The protest out of Eastern Europe was that in our shared worship services an appropriate place should also be granted to music styles that reflect the Eastern European tradition and experience. Adjustments were attempted immediately, and a reasonable measure of understanding was reached.

Our tour in 1989 with the Piatochas and thirty-five others was primarily to churches in Ukraine. The statistics they shared as to churches and church membership were not radically different from those of the entire Canadian Baptist Federation at that same time, something in the order of 1,300 churches with about 130,000 baptized members. Theological institutions had not been allowed to function. One paused to marvel at the grace of God as seen in the functioning of the church leadership, whose preparation had been largely experiential rather than academic. I noted that at Rovno, west of Kiev, Pastor Boris Krischuk was responsible for more than fifty churches with a total membership of about 5,000. Still farther west, around Lutzk, Pastor Jakob Kravchenko had oversight of eighty-two churches and an additional twenty-one congregations. And so it went.

Parallel with the pastors' and workers' conference to which I was bringing Bible studies and keynote themes, there was a gathering of the pastors' wives. Incredible as it may seem, they had never before met together collectively. They knew each other by ones and twos, but any conference gathering for them was totally unknown. Virginia was one of the keynote speakers at this conference. She speaks of her sense of awe at having this unique privilege, sharing the input responsibility with Mary Piatocha and with the wives of senior Ukrainian pastors.

Our tour of Russia and Ukraine was not characterized by a lot of humour. We were dealing with people who had come through a long struggle for survival, for their very existence. They took their life and their faith very seriously. Humour, at least our style of humour, does not seem to have been one of their survival devices.

Contrasts with experiences from other continents brought us a smile from time to time. For instance, our Congolese and Angolan students at Sona Bata had all been multicultural and multilingual. Flexibility and adaptability were among their strongest characteristics. Those African high school students all spoke three or more languages. In fact, one of my students spoke seven languages from four radically different language families. Many people we met in Ukraine were unicultural and unilingual, resisting to a degree even the use of Russian, a related language which, from our point of view, should not be too difficult for them to learn or at least to understand. Against this background we were told of the query concerning us which someone brought to Alex Piatocha. We made it our quote of the day: "How come these visitors talk so clear and plain, but we can't understand them?"

The conference that was the centrepiece of our tour took place at the newly constructed Swatoshina Baptist Church in Kiev. In fact, we shared in the dedication services for that new place of worship. There was no indication that I would have any special participation, but years of travel in churches away from Western Europe and North America had taught me to be prepared. The night before, I located a passage from Second Chronicles, chapter seven, that would be appropriate as a dedication message, and had a number of concepts briefly outlined in my Bible, developing the theme. On the morning of the dedication we went early enough to get a seat, and were comfortably installed in the third or fourth row from the front. A messenger came looking for me. Alex and I were to follow him to the preparation room behind the platform, there to be informed that I was the main speaker of the morning.

With a choir of one hundred voices and a twenty-five-piece orchestra, the music was worthy of such an event. Although this dedication took place under *glasnost*, the preparations had been undertaken under the harsh eye and hand of a previous, hostile regime. There are endless stories that will never be told; we heard only hints of the hardships. Church construction had proceeded ahead of the official permission, which had been sought year after year. At one juncture Baptists of Kiev were tipped off secretly that their new place of worship, still under construction, was to be bulldozed on a Monday morning. They rushed ahead over the weekend to put a roof in place. The law provided for the demolition of buildings only up to the point where the roof was in place. They managed to pass that hurdle on the weekend, and by doing so they saved their place of worship.

Events like this dedication drew a huge attendance, predictably double the available seating in this very large church. Cultural background and expectations made it much easier for the congregation to be patient while having to stand through services, even long ones. In the Russian and Ukrainian Orthodox Churches, seating was not part of the arrangement. It is considered normal to stand through worship. Seating, when available, is an extra, probably provided for the elderly and the infirm.

In fact, only a standing or kneeling position is considered worthy and appropriate for prayer, whether public or private. When one leads in public prayer the congregation stands, whether or not they are invited to do so. This arrangement often results in several uncomfortable situations before a visiting speaker from the West readjusts his practice of how prayer happens. A brief, spontaneous prayer, especially a "sentence prayer," cannot be lightly inserted into a meeting where attendance runs to several thousand people, a meeting conducted through translation. At least one full sentence is pronounced prior to any translation, then the translation also takes its time. At that point the congregation, however vast, will begin to rise—an action that may involve ten seconds or more. All this tends to make formal prayer yet more formal and deliberate than in many other countries.

In Borislav, south of L'viv we heard more detail of just how difficult it had been, before *glasnost* and *perestroika*, to secure construction permission and then to build. For twelve years they worked on the documentation requesting permission to build.

"In that time we buried three national leaders and three leaders in the Department of Religious Affairs."

When permission was granted, the site assigned to them was a swampy property on a side street, considered unusable. Details of the building process were translated for us. They began by moving hundreds of tons of fill to make the site usable, a highly labour-intensive project involving

Natalya Margola leads the choir and orchestra at Borislav, Ukraine. She mixed and carried cement for construction of this new church building.

men, women and children. There were no private construction companies to be hired, and of course they had no access to government building teams or equipment. Those who worked regular day shifts donated their evenings and nights for the project.

"At first we had no insomnia, but later we became very tired and found it difficult to sleep." They described how work went so well and so fast that non-Christians from other parts of the town would detour by the site on their way home from work, just to see the miracle of what had been accomplished the night before.

This new church construction which we visited at Borislav was so stunning that I pursued details on how it was accomplished. Women mixed, by hand, and carried all the cement, even the cement used to pour the high, vaulted ceiling. Men poured it into the forms and added the elaborate decorative work. Although this and other newly constructed churches tended to have a massive appearance, sometimes almost barn-like, on the outside, the interior was always highly ornate.

We gathered, bit by bit, the personal history of one remarkable lady who directed the choir, but who had also been part of that hard-working cement crew. Her appearance was striking, bordering on elegant, and one sensed that she was a woman of culture. Calling for a translator and requesting a bit of her background, we learned the following.

"I had an opportunity to study in Poland, and graduated with a degree as an economic engineer. . . . I found employment; then three times I was discharged, because of my Christian faith. . . . I have experienced no sadness or tragedy in my life, only persecution for my Lord."

The above was shared with a gentle warmth, a smile, no hint of a martyr complex. Work, faithfulness, sacrifice, artistic music were all natural components of her life being lived to honour her Lord Jesus.

Throughout this tour we could sense daily changes in the political climate. Leaders told us of experiences that would have been unthinkable only a month or two earlier. Some ledger entries:

"Yesterday I took part in a public debate with a prominent atheist, [whose name was cited]. We presented the approach of each position to questions of morality." The speaker went on to say that the debate was held in the city's planetarium, a worker there having proposed such a debate to his director.

"We recently conducted a service in a jail with about 1,200 inmates, repeat criminals. Half of them came to the service. There were many tears." Pastor Jakob Duchonchenko, who related these events, referred to that day among prisoners as one of the most rewarding of his life. He mentioned to the prisoners that he had been interned himself as a prisoner in the 1950s because of his faith. With the warden's agreement he set up ongoing personal encounters with inmates. A prisoner wanted to kiss his hand. He responded, "No, but I will kiss you."

Bold, young church leaders just emerging into pastoral roles exploited some of the opportunities of those transitional weeks. One such story was told by regional Pastor Matveev of L'viv.

"I said to him, 'Fedya, why do you rent a stadium when you have only fifty-five old people in your congregation?' Yet about five hundred peo-

Grigori Komendant continues as a key leader among Ukrainian Baptist churches, having been active earlier throughout the former USSR.

ple turned up. Fedya told us that he advertised on *The Liar* [the collective farmers' radio]. He also commented that a red-hat policeman was present at the meeting. The officer corrected a drunk and stopped someone from smoking. It was amazing that these police, who for years had been their terror, could actually be helpful."

In L'viv the blue and yellow flag of Ukraine flying in the city square caused a buzz among the Ukrainians travelling with us. When we could find a quiet moment we learned from Alex that this was the very first day in contemporary history that anyone had dared to fly the Ukrainian flag, and they did so with impunity.

History was happening around us; we were present to see the cracks of disintegration of a system that was crumbling. For those of us who have grown up in North America it is not easy to grasp the profound implications of living as a persecuted minority. There are lessons to be learned, valuable contributions toward true freedom and tolerance in our own society. Breakfast conversations that week painted the picture of how, in Czarist times, the Orthodox priest controlled each rural village in conjunction with the police, the gravedigger and any other important people. There was simply no latitude for freedom either in life or in death. Baptists who had grown up under this regime made comments to us such as these: "The gospel was being preached in Germany. Our people had to be sent there as prisoners to hear it."

In the airport on our way out of Moscow Virginia was seized by some form of food poisoning. To add to her discomfort, our plane was delayed and no seating was available in the airport. She simply sat on the floor as we waited. The ultimate cancellation of the flight involved an additional night in Moscow. In time buses came to take us to a small hotel somewhere in the suburbs for a rest between 11 p.m. and 4 a.m. We experienced a certain amount of tension over whether we would make the morning flight, especially since we were delayed by a member of our own group in the room next to ours. We had learned of her sleeping habits as we travelled. To begin with, she was quite hard of hearing. In addition, she used ear plugs, wrapped her head in a towel and covered her upper ear with a pillow. It was an embarrassing exercise to stand in the corridor of a public hotel at four-thirty in the morning, pounding on a door and shouting. We made the flight.

My later experience in the same Moscow airport occurred as I took Professor Dr. Harold Dressler of Vancouver on his introductory visit to Russia and the Commonwealth of Independent States (CIS). By this time Virginia and I were living at Miloslavov, near Bratislava in Slovak Republic. Harold was becoming more and more frustrated with his lack of invitations to conduct the teaching sessions for which he had come to Europe. I was happy to schedule a needed visit to the Russian Republic in a way that would allow me to introduce Harold to institutions requesting help, notably seminaries and Bible schools. When we flew into Moscow's Sheremetyevo airport I fully expected there would be someone there to meet us, in response to the series of fax messages I had sent, some of which were even acknowledged. All of them had gone through to their destinations.

For some reason I find Sheremetyevo to be one of the world's most intimidating airports, something like Kinshasa. That is especially true in

Harold Dressler (with beard) confers with church leaders at Bryansk, Russia.

Moscow when one is not accompanied by someone who speaks the language and knows the ropes. Harold and I cleared customs and immigration, got our baggage, then scanned the ranks in the arrivals hall of those who were awaiting incoming passengers. We declined the many offers of transportation, and settled down to wait for those who would surely be there to meet us.

My assurances to Harold grew less and less confident as each half-hour interval rolled by. Leaving Harold to guard the luggage, I unlocked the mysteries of the pay-phone system through a series of discussions at various boutiques. I then began working my way through the eight or nine phone numbers listed in my little black book. In one way or another each call was unsuccessful. Sometimes I reached the sound of a voice speaking only Russian. Sometimes it was that variety of beeps and tones that a only phone system can come up with, signals that vary from country to country. By whatever signs and signals, we were back at point zero.

Hours passed, boutiques closed, we came close to being the only people around, and it became more and more evident that we were on our own. I negotiated with a taxi driver the precise fare that he would charge to find us a hotel with a vacancy, and to take us there. The secret seems to be that one must always negotiate the fare with finality before getting in the cab. This time it worked. Once we were safely checked into the hotel it was time to switch from the nervous laugh to a genuine shared chuckle about the experience.

As a result of that trip Harold's contacts blossomed into a full-blown program of teaching and ministry, to which he continues to recruit additional participants. Six years later he is still operating this program from his base in the greater Vancouver area. The stories Harold has garnered in the interim make all of the above sound very tame and routine.

Harold and I got a night's sleep, then made our way mid-morning to Moscow Baptist Church and the offices, in that same building, that served as denominational headquarters. Finally we understood why we had not been met. The office was utterly swamped with the dozens of parachurch organizations rushing to open work in what was still the U.S.S.R., all using this one contact address. The dozens of organizations launching their ventures in the former Soviet Union soon became hundreds.

While living near Bratislava in 1992 I made a naive beginning at researching the names of such organizations, hoping I might identify which were genuine, and to what degree. Some, it seems, were largely a front for fund-raising operations, primarily for the benefit of the organizer. It soon became evident that there were well over 3,000 organizations operating in Eastern Europe. A significant portion of those seemed to make their beginnings through the churches that had survived the Communist era. I later concluded that even this estimate was much too conservative. My research efforts were eventually abandoned.

Harold and I sat in the waiting room as that morning's batch of delegations came through, were received and processed. After that we were warmly and apologetically received by the few overworked and baffled

Alex Piatocha chats with church members outside their new place of
worship at Zitomir, Ukraine.

people doing their best to handle a situation that was rapidly becoming
overwhelming. There were moments when I wondered whether our visit
was a mistake, unneeded. They assured us that we had a special place
because we were "family," and teaching was needed. At their suggestion, we proceeded by train that very night to Bryansk, where we made a
series of discoveries. Harold was walking into his chosen niche, and it
was the beginning of meaningful ministries for him.

In Bryansk Harold and I learned much of the people's history, the
suffering, the victories of faith and prayer. We were also impressed with
the dedication of Christians and their congregational leaders, facing challenges such as the human disasters arising from the Chernobyl nuclear
meltdown. Mature and experienced men whose emotions were not easily shaken were moved to tears as they told us of children growing up
without teeth, as a result of the children's own exposure or of their mothers' pre-natal exposure to radiation.

A ledger note for December 7, 1991, reminds me that the BBC newscast announced that on the seventieth anniversary of the Bolshevik revolution, the Russian parliament had issued a decree abolishing the Communist Party. That week we were in temporary residence at Miloslavov, Slovakia, near Bratislava, due to the uncertainties surrounding the Serb/Croat conflict.

Over the next four years we lived on the outer fringe of what we had come to know as the Soviet Bloc. We noted that the reverberations of events taking place in the Russian Republic were constantly sending shock waves through neighbouring countries. Residents of these other countries were left open-mouthed at the extent, the speed and the impact of the radical changes in Russia. During that four-year period we also observed the early signs of a widespread disillusionment related to work, food and the false expectations that an easy life should somehow be just around the corner.

"What's the use of giving the dog a longer chain if you move his bowl back out of reach?" This was a common saying among Russians and Ukrainians at the time.

Eastern Europeans had developed a widespread acceptance of conditions under which daily life was predictable, with mostly enough of the basics most of the time. The economic and material benefits of the new political order did not keep pace with expectations, and there were probably lots of people in the background actively feeding the discontent. This swelled to become a popular backlash, at least a widespread verbal grumbling. Considerably more value was being placed on what should happen materially and economically than on freedoms of expression, decision, worship, and movement. The populations expected that a move to the famed democracy would bring instant riches without the need to work for them.

At no time did we actually live in the U.S.S.R. or in the Commonwealth of Independent States, which emerged from it. However, we related to it and interacted with churches there directly in a number of ways. The events we experienced in republics of the former U.S.S.R. left a lasting impression. The overall effect of the changes accompanying *perestroika* and the subsequent collapse of Communism definitely fall within the category of remarkable events which we saw as being a very evident part of God's working.

12
Albania
Bread for the masses

Our first contacts with Albania were made from Dubrovnik in what was then Yugoslavia. This put us no more than one hundred and fifty kilometres from the most northerly tip of Albania on the Adriatic coast. But Albania was in a totally different world politically. Albania had stood for decades as the most closed country on the face of the earth. It was closed politically, commercially and religiously. The Communist dictator, Enver Hoxha, had made every effort to seal off Albania from the outside world. Albanians were not permitted to travel or to emigrate. Those who attempted to do so were often shot, or drowned in their attempt to swim to Italy. Anyone caught attempting to flee Albania was subject to a long prison sentence at hard labour. Even then, one was not necessarily released when the sentence had been served.

From a religious point of view, Albania was even more isolated. It was officially declared to be an atheistic nation, with no form of religion practised or tolerated. For the most part churches and mosques had been bulldozed. A few were left as museums or cultural heritage sites, but not as places of worship. Statistics from the 1930s, just prior to the Communist regime, listed the population as seventy percent Muslim, eighteen percent Orthodox and twelve percent Roman Catholic. By the time of our arrival in Dubrovnik, Albania had been deprived of any outward form of religious practice for some forty-five years. Implementation of the prohibition had been so severe that they succeeded in foiling any attempt at maintaining an underground church.

In this context Virginia and I studied the tourist brochure posted by Atlas Tours of Dubrovnik, advertising their two-day bus tour into Albania. With *glasnost* exercising its effect on other parts of Eastern Europe, it seems that even Albania was influenced. By 1990, controlled bus tours were allowed. Canadians fell within the category of those who could visit, whereas Americans could not. We signed up for this tour on our tenth day in Dubrovnik, and travelled to Albania via Titograd in Montenegro just one week later.

Our tour guide John Krga established very strict rules for his participants. No photos were allowed except where and when he indicated – and never photos of military sites, bunkers, or uniforms. We must take absolutely no printed material of any form with us. Presumably passports and money would be his two exceptions. This meant of course that we were not allowed to take a Bible or any portion of Scripture. We discussed the many stories we had heard of people smuggling Bibles into the Soviet Union, but opted to go with the rules according to Krga, praying only that God would give us one meaningful contact through this visit to Albania.

That meaningful contact was to be Gilbert. He and another guide, Julia, boarded our bus at the border. Tour bus guides came only in the plural form, instructed to watch each other and report on suspicious activities or contacts. They followed a scripted text, and had been prepared in advance with answers for most questions that might arise, such as the role of religion in Albania. For much of two days they were with us. At each stop there was a commentary.

We placed ourselves so that as we returned to the bus or walked on to the next site, we were next to Gilbert. We fished for little bits of personal information from him. He was married. He had an infant daughter. He was an English teacher, and lived in Tirana. These bits of information emerged slowly, and in a guarded moment he wrote his address in my notebook. Only years later did I learn from Gilbert that sharing his ad-

Gilbert was our first Albanian contact. He and his wider family became our firm friends.

dress would have cost him fifteen to twenty-five years in prison if Julia had seen and reported it.

Statistics and a specific edited version of history were made available to us in abundance. This was a country of 20,000 square miles, with a population of three million. We learned of the Turkish occupation beginning in the fourteenth century, and of Albania's national hero, Skanderbek, who liberated them from Turkish rule. After Skanderbek, Turkey ruled again until 1912. After a few decades of independence Albania was then occupied by Italy and Germany from 1939 to 1944. Our guides spoke of independence and single-party rule beginning in 1949. The "founder" Hoxha ruled until his death in 1985 and was followed by President Ramiz Alia, still in power as we made that tour. The guides weighed certain words carefully, speaking of "steps toward democratization" that were now being taken by their country.

Our eyes told us more than we learned from our tour guides. The buildings were dullness personified, apart from a few public structures near the city centre. The country looked and felt exceedingly poor. There was no private ownership of vehicles. In two full days of travel we saw one motor car. It was a Volvo owned by the Swedish Ambassador. Single-lane paved roads permitted troops to be rushed anywhere. Our bus met trucks from time to time. Either one vehicle would make way completely, or they would strike a compromise by each keeping one set of wheels on the pavement.

We observed a very drab country in which paint seemed to be unknown. Clearly the World Development Map taped to my office wall was skewed, as it had shown Albania (with all other Communist countries) as being fully developed. A more realistic evaluation of Albania in 1990 would place it closer to Angola on the economic scale. The most striking feature of the countryside had to be the presence of the military bunkers. They were a beehive shape, built of reinforced concrete and partially buried in the ground. The country had something over 700,000 of them, built at roughly the same unit cost as the meagre apartments, which were named *pallati*—palace.

Public symbols representing Communism were prominent. Bronze statues of Marx and Lenin faced each other across the boulevard that leads from Tirana's central square to the parliament buildings. Our bus stopped there to allow for photos, but there were no takers. I regret not recording their presence for they were soon to become obsolete. In the town square itself stood a prominent statue of Enver Hoxha, and we do have a record of that.

Albania had already gone through two separate Communist alliances, first with Russia then, after alienation, with China. The Russians in their era had carved a submarine base into the side of a mountain that rose vertically from the sea on the southern outskirts of Vlore. The mark of the Chinese Communist era was the chemical smelting complex at Elbasan. The technology for these foundries was so archaic and so polluting that there is a story in circulation that as the Chinese were withdrawing, the head engineer at Elbasan sent an enquiry to China. "Do we sabotage the works at Elbasan, or do we leave them intact?" He was

very large segment of
the population on the street, parents walking with children, often hand in
hand. The atmosphere was totally peaceful, in fact it was quite eerie in
the degree of silence. We later learned that this quiet turnout of the population walking the streets, was the wildest form of protest allowed by the
totalitarian government—but it was indeed a protest.

After our return to Dubrovnik two significant events relating to Albania happened before Christmas. Gilbert, our one meaningful contact, sent
us a greeting on a plain post card. It was not a Christmas card as such, but
its arrival coincided with Christmas. That made us wonder whether this
man who had made so many pronouncements against religion as a tour
guide might have a different opinion in private.

The second event was the complete collapse of Albanian Communism, virtually without a death-struggle. The population continued to
gather on the streets, and became bolder. The ultimate in symbolism happened when the statues of Lenin, Marx and Hoxha were all pulled down.
Communism had collapsed in Albania virtually overnight, and the country was in transition.

Less than a month after the collapse of Communism in Albania Virginia and I flew from Dubrovnik to Vienna for a meeting that became the
turning point in our European assignment. The connection to Albania
was that Karl Heinz Walter, general secretary of the European Baptist
Federation (EBF), took a special interest in our recent trip to Albania. He
began inquiring about the possibility that I would set up a visit for him
and a group of colleagues, to explore the possibilities of undertaking
work there on behalf of the EBF. To my regret, eleven months would
pass before that wish was realized. The beginnings of war in Yugoslavia
were a distraction, including our own removal to residence in the Slovak
Republic. We were busy evaluating whether Canadian Baptists should
be involved in programs in Bulgaria, Romania, Poland, the Baltic states
or elsewhere.

Rapid changes were taking place throughout Eastern Europe during the summer of 1991. My ledger entry for August 24 reads: *Today's political events continue at the stunning pace typical of this week. Gorbachev has resigned as party general secretary. He recommends dismantling the party. Individual republics are nationalizing party property. Estonia and the Ukraine have declared their independence.* The U.S.S.R. was disintegrating. There seemed to be a lot of ministry options open; priority decisions were required.

I began to work on getting visas to facilitate the visit Karl had suggested. In late August, from our temporary base in Vienna, I located the Vienna Embassy of the Albanian Republic. I remember standing across the street and prayerfully studying the white building behind a black iron fence, its shutters all closed, showing no external signs of life. Interesting developments were to take place there, but I had no way of knowing that. There was a buzzer at the iron gate with one of those small communications boxes. When one pressed the buzzer it would be appropriate to be prepared with at least a mental line of approach. On August 26, when I studied the embassy, I had not yet developed that concept.

Throughout our Eastern European assignment, stretching from the end of September 1990 to the end of December 1995, Virginia and I became increasingly conscious that God was opening doors of ministry and service that we ourselves would not have been able to open through strategic planning. Nowhere was that focus stronger than in a long string of what some would call coincidental events that resulted in the beginnings of an Albanian work that came to be known as the European Baptist Federation Albania Program.

In October Karl Heinz Walter phoned a couple of times to discuss possible dates for a visit to Albania by a number of us representing several agencies. I went to the Albanian Embassy for preliminary contacts that might lead to visas. I had nothing more strategic planned than to ask what language we might use in communication, since I don't speak German. With a considerably heightened pulse rate I pressed that buzzer on the box by the steel gate. Instead of hearing a fuzzy voice through the box, a door of the embassy opened. At least I was dealing with an individual!

Maxim Sinnemati was first secretary at Albania's embassy in Vienna. It was he who released the embassy's outer gate when I buzzed. I asked in careful English what language we could use, since I don't speak German. His answer came with a smile, "I don't speak German either. Why don't we use English?" He had never met a Canadian, and it seems that he wanted a friendship. Our discussions were informal, around an oval coffee table. I was puzzled at his excellent use of English, and inquired about it. He had learned English secretly at night, listening to news broadcasts of the BBC World Service. Had he been discovered it would have meant prison or worse.

I explained my desire to set up a visit for as many as six to eight people of various nationalities, and that as Baptists we wanted to help Albania through its time of transition into modern Europe. His question was a bit surprising.

"Are you all Baptists?"

Yes, all Baptists.

"You will have no problems with visas, I will assure that." We had made a beginning, and I departed with the necessary forms to be filled in by whoever was to take part in this delegation.

At some point in October or November it became evident that neither Karl Heinz nor the others who had hoped to travel with us could make the time free in their calendars. Virginia and I were asked to undertake this visit alone, as representatives of the European Baptist Federation. My ledger reveals a November 25 breakthrough in making the travel arrangements, then a final booking on November 28 through Budapest. There was no precedent to go by; all attempts were by trial and error through travel agencies in Vienna, crossing from Bratislava to Albania by train. From a fax later sent to Toronto, this quote:

The signs were not good as we prepared to go in. We could get in, but could get no confirmed flights out. Not very encouraging, but confirmation came at the last minute. Then, the day before the flight we learned that the government had collapsed. Would it be possible to make contacts? Would there be civil disorder? How seriously should we take our inability to get confirmed hotel bookings, and where should we stay? We still felt led to proceed.

On December 4 Mr. Sinnemati at the Albanian Embassy in Vienna was as good as his word, and we received our visas without problem, and free of charge at that. Perhaps pushing our luck a bit, I emphasized that our travel agent was unable to confirm hotel arrangements for us in Tirana. Would he make a request to his ministry there, asking that arrangements be made for us, including someone to meet us at the airport? This was hardly a standard request by one seeking to initiate mission work in a country that had been closed for half a century. He said he would try.

Rumours were rife of food shortages in Albania, so we purchased some items like salami, cheese and figs to take as gifts. On the flight we began to pick up the first horror stories of how life had been under the Hoxha regime. A fellow passenger was returning to Albania for the first time since fleeing the country eight years earlier. Tony was now twenty-eight and working in Detroit. His escape had involved eight hours of swimming in the Adriatic. His companion had died of a heart attack only a few hundred metres from safety on the Italian shore.

As we undertook this second visit Virginia and I were not aware of even a single Albanian believer worshipping in any of the world's religions, Christian or otherwise. We later learned that in Kosovo (a part of Yugoslavia where there is a heavy concentration of Albanians), Swedish Pentecostals had begun to work among Albanian-speaking people, as had a Serbian Baptist Pastor, Simo Ralevic. When Albania's Communist regime fell, these and others did not delay the transfer of efforts to Albania itself. Our contacts were developed independently. When doctors Chris and Mairi Burnett moved to Albania as pioneers of the EBF Albania work they picked up on the serious networking with other organizations.

My memories of Tirana airport on December 5, 1991, are still strong. The patrols, whether army or police, carried automatic weapons and wore rumpled uniforms that looked as though the soldiers' mothers had made them. A few solitary light bulbs of low wattage hung on long cords from the airport ceiling. Whether or not other passengers were tense I don't

Albania's serious food shortages following independence led to food lines in Tirana.

know, but I can assure you that we were. We had prayed much about this visit, which we considered significant, and we felt that much was at stake. The men carrying the guns eyed all of us suspiciously, and there was mostly stillness as we edged forward in line to have passports examined.

I held our two Canadian passports tilted so the curious could see where we were from. We heard "Canada" whispered up the line. A man appeared who called out in French, "Where are the Canadians?" He had come to meet us at the request of the Ministry of Foreign Affairs, in response to the fax from Mr. Sinnemati at their Vienna Embassy. This man meeting us, Bardhyl Fico, was the recently appointed political secretary for the Muslim religion in Albania. Bardhyl took our passports, asked us to sit at the side while he did the VIP treatment on documents. He had arranged a car that would take us to Tirana, and had booked a room for us in the Hotel Arberia at US$40 per night.

The moment Bardhyl greeted us both with courtesy—and me with an embrace—the most remarkable twelve days of our entire career began.

Albania appointed three secretaries of religion following independence. Bardhyl (right) opened doors to consult with government ministries.

Before our baggage was unloaded from the plane he asked directly, "Why have you come?"

Our preparations had been deliberate, and prayer intense. Karl Heinz Walter had repeatedly expressed hope that we could make direct contact with officials of the transitional government. That was the approach on which we were building, tested first at the Albanian Embassy in Vienna. We wanted to establish extensive government contacts with various ministries, and find out if there were areas in which specific skills and experience were needed and desired. In response to Albanian government requests we would attempt to draw personnel from Baptist resources around the world, either as volunteers or career workers. So when Bardhyl asked his question it was easy to be open and direct.

"Tomorrow we would like to go to the Ministry of Agriculture." We explained a bit of our rationale. The response was just as immediate and just as direct.

"I'll go with you."

From my ledger the following note: *Locating our luggage, Bardhyl ushered us past the mass of people, running suitcases through the X-Ray to guard against an arms shipment, but waving aside all other inquiries. At the exit the mass of humanity waiting for relatives was a real tangle. But Bardhyl and the driver Regep Lika, together with guide Denisa Daka, shepherded us into a red Volkswagen Passat station wagon for our prestige run to town. Pride was very much at stake. A beige Mercedes dared to pass us on the dark road. Honour had been slighted. Over the next few kilometres Regep finally managed to pass the Mercedes again, and so his honour remained intact.*

It was a scary ride.

We spent perhaps the coldest nights of our lives in the Arberia Hotel. The hotel might have had heating on some occasion in the distant past, but certainly not recently. The city was undergoing what people described as its coldest spell in decades. Virginia and I went to bed fully clothed, shoes the single exception. Unfortunately the Arberia had no other saving graces to make up for its lack of warmth. Well, yes, it did offer shelter.

The following morning at eight Bardhyl was there to begin on foot our tour of the various government ministries. I recollect a pattern of approach that was to be repeated with remarkable precision. At the door of a ministry Bardhyl would pause, straighten his coat, strike a stance of dignity and poise, knock with authority then lead us into the reception area. It was always he who spoke.

"We want to speak with the minister."

"The minister is busy."

"Then get rid of whoever is with him, I have a delegation from the European Baptist Federation."

This opener never failed to get us a direct audience, not even once. In twelve days the ministries included agriculture, health, education, foreign affairs, food, mines and resources, international relations, Bardhyl's own Ministry of Sports, Culture and Religion, as well as one other influential standing committee functioning at the ministerial level. The programs that would eventually be established by the European Baptist Federation's Albania Committee grew, for the most part, out of these initial contacts, but were given much more substantial content once workers were appointed who came to live and work full time in Albania.

At the Ministry of Food we encountered protesters; a hungry population crowded around the front gate. We were allowed to push through the milling people, Bardhyl at the point of our wedge. We have no record of what he told the protesters, perhaps that these foreigners were part of the solution. This background of an angered population in the streets continued, however, throughout our trip. One loud and angry column seemed to be coming from the main square to the ministry itself. Our pulses quickened. They made their protest and moved on, and our pulse went back to normal. Those were very tense days. On December 10 thirty-five men were trampled and burned to death in a riot at a food storage depot. We passed by the burned-out shell of the building just two days later—and in a vehicle of the Ministry of Foreign Affairs. It was not the best of times to be travelling under government auspices.

On that first visit to the ministry Albania's food situation was put before us plainly: the country was down to a five-day reserve of food. Would Canada be able to do anything about that? We were prepared to try. This was more than a year before I began using electronic mail, so fax messages were still the backbone of our communications. The Ministry of Food had its own fax machine and they would transmit any inquiry I might draft.

We made our appeal to The Sharing Way, the relief and development arm of Canadian Baptist Ministries. I carried both laptop computer and printer with me on this as on other trips. I drafted a summary and sent it off to Canada. The needs of the country were cited as 100,000 tonnes of wheat per month from January through June. Whatever Baptists could provide would be only a token contribution.

The return fax from The Sharing Way appended the application forms to be filled out by anyone applying for food from the Canadian Foodgrains Bank. It was so extensive that I stretched it out on the floor to pace off its length—fifteen metres. The Albanians' first reaction was to be overwhelmed by this foreign documentation rivalling what a Communist regime might demand. In the end that paper work was a blessing because it established the first working relationship between us and one of Albania's government departments. We found a large table and sat down to work systematically through the questions relating to criteria, decision making, transportation, storage, distribution, and reporting. Functionaries even came to our hotel room at night to double check items needing clarification.

The result was a shipment of wheat flour, with The Sharing Way serving as initiator and partial contributor, and the Canadian Foodgrains Bank implementing the shipment. Major contributions came through the Baptist World Alliance from multiple sources including Southern Baptists. The latter sent Mike Creswell as a professional photographer to document arrival and delivery. Dozens of communications, many phone calls and a number of adventures would intervene before that flour would be safely delivered to the warehouses and bakeries of Tirana. Another trip to Albania was required to finalize arrangements. Just when we thought everything was arranged, the shipping date was changed. The new arrival date was a Saturday morning – not an auspicious time, but we were assured that port authorities and longshoremen would be on hand to clear the shipment.

Saturday morning arrived. The ship arrived. The port was closed. The ship proceeded north along the coast and unloaded at the nearest available port, which happened to be in Montenegro (Yugoslavia). Our precious cargo of wheat flour was now in a foreign country, and a country engaged in hostilities at that.

Mike Creswell or others could give a more detailed account of what happened next, but I heard it this way. A convoy of Albanian trucks was arranged to pick up the flour in Montenegro. Shortly after crossing back into Albania they were halted by armed bandits, to whom both the trucks and the flour were equally appealing. A courageous little Albanian truck driver, described as something of a ruffian with a ferocious tongue became our hero of the day. He took a stance, and held to it tenaciously.

"You can get these keys by shooting me. Don't bluff me, just go ahead and shoot—otherwise you'll get no keys from me." He was eventually told that his courage had saved him, that he and his other drivers should take their trucks and go. Mike Creswell's photos recorded the unloading of flour in Tirana as the bakeries went to work. The eventual result was bread available to the public, and it seems to have made a difference in Albania's first hard winter.

Our most prized contact at the Ministry of Foreign Affairs became Rudolf Marku, director of a department within the ministry. Rudolf was known throughout Albania as a resistance poet and a patriot. These credentials won him an appointment in the interim government. Of all those whom we met, Rudolf became the most eloquent spokesman for the agonies and atrocities suffered by his people under the Hoxha regime. On two occasions in his apartment we met people who had been arrested and imprisoned for decades for infractions as insignificant as trying to visit the neighbouring country.

Later Rudolf would be elected as deputy to parliament, representing the District of Lezhe. It was Rudolf who would stand up in the National Assembly to argue in favour of freedom of religion for Albania. On the day I presented him with a full Bible (in English) in the lobby of the Hotel Tirana, Rudolf stood with tears in his eyes, palms upward with the Bible resting as a treasured object on both hands.

"I've always wanted to have this book. It has the Psalms of David." On a later visit Rudolph commented, "You know, I'm reading all the Bible, not just the Psalms."

One of our visits in the Ministry of Foreign Affairs took a remarkable twist. While Rudolf himself was very open, a certain secretary who assisted him had been looking at us from under his frown. He eventually voiced a question that had been building.

"Did you come here to help our people, or did you come here to bring your religion?"

The moment was a tense one, but I thanked him for an excellent question, which opened up quite naturally the whole topic of our motivation. I explained that for those of us who call ourselves Baptist, the model is Jesus. I produced a New Testament and gave it to him for study, suggesting that beginning from a certain page number (here I indicated Luke's Gospel, chapters four through twelve), he should attempt to decipher for himself exactly what Jesus was busy doing. Was Jesus helping people in a practical way, or was he proclaiming the kingdom of God? My affirmation was that Jesus regularly left one unfinished, to move to the other. In Jesus, witness and service were integrated.

"That is what we have come to Albania to do. We want to help Albanian people in a practical way. We also believe that faith in Jesus provides a moral fabric for a nation, important to its well-being." This answer seems to have been satisfactory. Months later this same man was walking the streets with us helping to search for the apartment where our first resident workers would live with their family.

Teuta was another remarkable acquaintance during these early days. She was a young mother, a gifted and articulate woman married to a medical doctor. She and her husband Muftar were first-hand observers of the remarkable events

Petrit was helpful as embassy chauffeur in Vienna. He introduced Virginia Keith to his daughter in a casual meeting on the street in Tirana.

that accompanied Albania's exit from the decades of Communism. Teuta described the scene in the square on the night of the first dramatic events. They saw a small boy with a rope shinny up the statue of former dictator Enver Hoxha. Police fired shots from a distance, but did not hit him. He was able to slip his rope through the arm of the statue, and tie it there. The crowd began to pull on the rope. I made notes then of Teuta's statements: *We thought that together all the people in the square would not be able to pull him down. . . . He came down so easily. . . . He was all empty inside. . . . We had been afraid of him for so long.*

Religion in that Albania of 1991 was beginning to function once again, after decades of being outlawed. It did so under the surveillance of the Ministry of Sports, Culture and Religion. We have followed closely the processes and people involved, for religious freedom has never been, and is still not, secure. Bardhyl Fico, as the politically appointed secretary for the Muslim religion, functioned in tandem with two counterparts: a secretary for Roman Catholicism and a secretary for Albanian

Orthodoxy. The three of them worked out of the same office. Only the rigours of Albania's proclaimed atheistic government under Enver Hoxha could have produced such closeness among Muslim, Catholic and Orthodox.

A series of crises has threatened religious freedom in Albania. Often it is triggered by some specific activity, which then elicits reference to the irritating multiplicity of the sects that have invaded the country, ranging from Hare Krishna and Scientology to Jehovah's Witnesses. Several attempts have been made to establish legislation that would curb and control religious activity.

President Jimmy Carter and his wife Rosalind visited Albania in September 1993. Carter interacted closely with President Sali Berisha, and may have been of assistance in keeping at least some measure of religious tolerance alive. The Carters' gracious visit of forty-five minutes to our very modest Baptist centre triggered a flurry of activity by Tirana's municipal workers. They cleaned up mounds of garbage on the street and relocated the taxis that clustered around our gate, making room for the Carter motorcade. On their arrival in Tirana an early stop was at a presidential palace along the avenue. Chris Burnett and I had secured permission to greet them just inside the palace entrance. The entourage from the American Embassy smiled as we did in response to President Carter's sense of humour. He shook our hands, then glanced around at the vast marble chamber of that official building and commented "I like your Baptist Centre."

By the time of a November 1995 visit to Albania, when Bob and Grace Berry accompanied us, another crisis in religious freedom was pending. At the request of the missionary community I again established contact with the three secretaries of religion. The result was a two-week visit to Canada and the U.S.A. in July 1996 at which time they were guests in our home. We then travelled with them to New York, Washington, Richmond and Williamsburg. Blair Clark of Canadian Baptist Ministries assisted me with the driving, and in hosting these men. The purpose was to broaden the base of experience of these men to serve their country better, to expose them to the process by which religious freedom had been established in the United States, and to help them to consider options other

President Jimmy Carter was helpful in working toward religious freedom in Albania. He and Rosalind visited the modest Baptist Centre in Tirana.

than religious legislation of a controlling nature. The results of these initiatives have been difficult to assess. The process of participating in them has been exhilarating.

An incident at the small international airport in Bratislava became symbolic of much that has happened with respect to Albania. We were living near Bratislava at the time. Our neighbour, Pastor Juraj Pribula picked me up at 4:30 a.m. for a flight to Zurich, where I would meet Keith Parker and Paul Thibodeaux to take them to Tirana. Pastor Pribula parked by the curb at the airport entrance in the pre-dawn hours. We waited and waited for signs of life at the airport where all appeared dark, the windows heavily tinted. Less than an hour before flight time there was still no sign of activity.

Leaving my luggage, I went up to the door to see if I could raise a response. The double doors slid wide, as did the set immediately beyond. All that was required was movement and the doors opened. Lack-

John Keith stands between Sultana, matriarch of the Romanies who live at Bregu, and her daughter Adelina, together with Armando. Armando was imprisoned after his attempt to defend his sister Adelina from abductors who would sell her in Italy.

ing motion, the doors stay perpetually closed. So many of our experiences relating to Albania had been like that—approach a door and it opens. Through this entire time we perceive God to have been the door opener to Albania.

Doctors Chris and Mairi Burnett, who had served in multiple capacities with the Baptist Missionary Society in Congo, became the residential pioneers of our EBF Albania Program. To introduce Chris and Mairi to our network of Albanian friends and acquaintances at many different levels was a delight. They were vigorous, energetic, had lots of initiative and lots of drive. They had a strong sense of God's call and leading in their lives, and a wealth of experience from Zaire, in addition to their medical training. With their residence established in Tirana a new era began and new relationships emerged. Chris and Mairi, with their two young boys, were the first of many who would be appointed from Britain, Italy, Sweden, the U.S.A. and Canada to live and work in Albania. Many were short-term volunteers, but there came to be about thirty in residence at a time, involved in programs of various kinds.

Until the end of 1995 I served as chair of the EBF Albania Committee, which met twice yearly in Tirana. Through this committee the various cooperating agencies met to establish policy, make major decisions and set direction for the joint work. From the end of 1995 Birgit Karlsson, a Swedish Baptist pastor, has chaired the committee.

Jonathan and Trish Steeper continue to minister in Tirana, 1995.

One of the milestones of those years took place in a room of the Hotel Tirana on September 20, 1992, with the first public worship service, attended by a number of prominent Albanians. In that first worship service the translator was Gilbert, the tour guide we had met nearly two years earlier on that initial bus tour into Albania from Dubrovnik. We were able to locate Gilbert's home before the end of our second visit, and our friendship has continued to grow ever since. Gilbert served as something of a secretary and counsellor to Chris Burnett; he helped us to locate the property that was to become our Baptist centre, and assisted in many ways with formalities. He helped the Albania committee regularly until he secured a position with the Ministry of Foreign Affairs. He rose in that post to become spokesman for his ministry, and was later appointed *chargé d'affaires* at the Albanian embassy in Rio de Janeiro. Virginia and I were seated with Gilbert and his wife Eva on the day Eva made her profession of faith, and I was present again on the day at the beach south of Durres when Eva and others were baptized.

It was also a memorable day when I was at Tirana's airport to meet Jonathan and Trish Steeper with their children, helping to establish them in their first apartment. This marked another phase of transition, as a new Canadian family was on hand to continue the links with Albania that Virginia and I had begun.

13
Croatia—Yugoslavia—Bosnia
Grace in hate-filled lands

Looking back on five years spent in Eastern Europe with Canadian Baptist Ministries we reach two immediate conclusions. First, those five years proved to be the most meaningful ones in a career spanning four decades. Second, the clear turning point that made this so came on the first day of the Gulf War, January 17, 1991.

By late November of 1990, signs of the pending Gulf War were building. Twice weekly an airline employee named Braco came to our Dubrovnik apartment as an unofficial language tutor in Croatian. The sentences we built together during each session became the following week's conversation starters with people on the street. "Saddam Hussein is a dangerous man." "He has stockpiles of chemical weapons." "He is killing his own people." "War in the Middle East could spread. . . ."

We arrived at Dubrovnik at the end of September 1990, when Croatia was still part of Yugoslavia. In a little over three months we had visited Albania as tourists and made an interesting exploratory trip through Belgrade into Bulgaria. Otherwise we remained close to home base, making local contacts and building foundations in the language. Within the year Dubrovnik was to become a centre of world interest and would be bombarded by more than 200,000 mortars, but on our arrival, that conflict was still in the future.

Historic Dubrovnik of little strategic value, sustained 200,000 mortar hits.

January 17, 1991 we were booked to fly to Zagreb and Vienna. Karl Heinz Walter, as general secretary of the European Baptist Federation, had convened a meeting of the North American representatives from several Baptist agencies, to meet in the Vienna apartment of Bob and Marilyn Fryckolm, representatives for American Baptist Churches. The flight was an early one. By long-established custom my alarm clock is set a few minutes before six. This permits me to monitor the BBC news on short wave while I shave. The bulletin of world news that morning announced that air strikes had been made into Iraq. The war soon to become known as "Desert Storm" was underway by about three hours.

Should we cancel or proceed with our plans? Would passenger flights be sabotaged? Would this escalate immediately into some wider conflict? The Balkan region where we were located was not very far from the Middle East; how would it be affected? There were other complications related to Virginia's lack of mobility as her right leg was in a cast. We prayed, deliberated, and went for it. Wheelchair service was available at Dubrovnik, then Zagreb and Vienna. It was a tense time, uncomfortable in more ways than one, but we experienced no unfavourable incidents. Circling over Vienna's Schwechat airport we saw an unusual cluster of identical aircraft. The entire fleet of Royal Jordanian Airlines had been flown to Vienna for safety, well away from the combat area in the Gulf.

In our short meeting that day a series of significant relationships were developed that would shape the next five years. We established friendship with Karl Heinz Walter, who planted in our minds the concept of making further contacts in Albania on behalf of the European Baptist Federation (EBF). Paul Thibodeaux of the Southern Baptist Foreign Mission Board would do more than any other to put us in touch with the entire range of Eastern European contacts. Harold Dressler would come to help fill in at Dubrovnik when we were back in Canada later in the year for deputation and consultations. Furthermore, I would take Harold on his introductory trip to the Russian Republic. Marilyn and Bob Fryckolm would open their Vienna home to us when the conflict between Croatia and Yugoslavia prohibited a return to Dubrovnik. It was a very significant day. How different those next five years would have been if we had made the "safe" decision not to fly on that first day of the Gulf War.

The move to Eastern Europe after twenty years in administration at CBM was neither a quick nor an easy decision. That much time in administration was enough, and we had been considering ministry in Brazil, which would not involve learning a new language. Both Wayne Larson, chair of CBM, and CBM board member Mark Parent had shared their convictions that this new departure could be beneficial in many ways, and they were right. Following a tour of several countries with Vlado Canji, pastor of a Yugoslavian Baptist congregation in Windsor, Ontario, and in response to a specific request from the Baptist Union of Yugoslavia, Virginia and I were on our way to Dubrovnik. We rented an apartment in Dubrovnik, with an outside room available for Bible studies and worship services.

Perhaps the most courageous decision of all was Virginia's willingness to pull up stakes again after twenty years of a more settled life in

Canada, and her willingness to undertake yet another language at age sixty, dependent upon two hearing aids. In a more reflective moment she confessed that she wasn't sure she could do it. She may have had doubts about herself, but nobody else doubted her capacity, and she certainly came through royally.

Judging only by the experiences of the three months prior to our Gulf War turning point, one would have to say we should have got back on the plane to return home. To start with, on the night of our arrival our landlady informed us that she had changed her mind about allowing the use of her annex room for meetings.

"You can't hold gatherings of people in my house."

She was too afraid of the authorities in a country that was still Communist. We had arrived at Dubrovnik's Konavle airport in the late afternoon and we were tired. Faced with this discouraging news, we simply went to bed for a night's rest, without even attempting to unpack.

I was awake before dawn. The priority item of business for this first day in Europe was to get the notebook computer switched over to two hundred and twenty volts, and operational for all communications. My handwriting is atrocious, which is why I had been carrying a portable typewriter everywhere for two decades. I removed the cover from the back of the computer, located the voltage control switch, then broke out in a cold sweat. It was already set on the two-twenty-volt option, not the one-ten-volt setting. But I had been using it constantly in Canada, and had not switched it to two-twenty. I dug the manual out of our luggage, carefully studied it, reviewed it again and again. Instructions were crystal clear. This change-over must be made, so I made it. From the next room Virginia heard the small explosion. The smell of ozone didn't linger too long, and the smoke soon cleared, to leave a fine black star-burst around the socket on the white wall. The breaker switch in the electrical panel was easy enough to reset, but the motherboard of my computer was irrevocably gone before we had eaten our first breakfast in Dubrovnik.

If there was any redeeming factor in that computer blowout it did not relate to efficiency, communications or a comfortable sense of being settled and at home. Probably it would be tied in with the tall men who worked in the customs office and the air freight department at the airlines. In Communist countries athletes were subsidized by the government by being placed in official work capacities and could thus maintain their amateur status in sports. These handsome giants were basketball players, and I got to meet a series of them in the process of shipping my computer back to Canada for repairs and then clearing it again when it was fixed. The most lasting friendship has been with Baldo Marić, and we still exchange Christmas greetings with Baldo and his wife Jasna.

During those early days at Dubrovnik we constantly encountered new and relevant topics for language study: "My wife fell on wet marble and broke her leg." "She was carrying a tea tray." "There were three serious breaks in the ankle." "They operated and put in screws." This accident happened on December 9, so Virginia never did get to see all of Dubrovnik on foot, which is the only way to get to know this beautiful little gem of a walled city beside the Adriatic, with its alleys, cobbled streets, walls that were built before Columbus sailed to America, and Onafrio's fountain dating from the eighth century.

The break happened on a Sunday night, just as a hurricane was building. Our landlady Milica was so shocked that this would happen on her patio that she made a serious attempt to force Virginia's foot back into position before we could stop her. The pain from that well-intended therapy was excruciating. Registration at the hospital wasn't too complicated. "Come in now, then look after details tomorrow." So they operated right away and registered Virginia the next day. Dr. Brailo, head of the hospital, had studied abroad, and was a good surgeon as well. We choose not to comment on his hospital's support system for post-operative care. By God's grace Dr. Brailo was on duty when we arrived by ambulance.

At that time the AIDS scare was a worldwide phenomenon. I insisted that if a blood transfusion were required I would be the donor. Virginia's blood type, A-, is rare, but we both carry the same type. I was brushed aside. "We don't need that." Nor, it seems, did they need to take blood pressure, though given Virginia's condition it would have been a wise move.

The following morning, with the hurricane now at full strength, I headed up to the hospital on foot in the heavy rain and lashing wind. It was a mistake to take my umbrella, but how could I be thinking clearly? There wasn't enough left of it to repair. After another block the wind whipped the glasses from my face. Although I don't see as well without them, I was still able to follow their progress, smooth as a puck across ice, until the wheel of a car caught one lens, popped the other and left me with something like a gold-coloured pretzel. Between there and the hospital the road crosses above the cove, a spot designated as the lovers' suicide cliff. The wind was particularly strong there, and the waves were crashing far below. Another pedestrian and I were caught by a particularly strong gust of wind. For one brief moment we locked arms, feet braced, in something less than a bear hug. It was enough to prevent being blown away. We smiled, nodded, then went our separate ways.

Nobody from the expatriate community had been known to opt deliberately for surgery in Yugoslavia. For the next couple of years Virginia found that their reaction was always one of unbelief. "What—you had the surgery in Dubrovnik?" But the surgery was well done, as affirmed by the Canadian specialist who eventually removed the screws.

"We might have used different hardware," was his comment. We are grateful to God for the eventual good results. As soon as possible Virginia was back in our apartment. That translates into four days. There was lots of motivation to acquire the basics of the language, though the nuances and the agreements were never mastered. During her recuperation Virginia was relocated to a bed in the small room where I had blown my computer. She claims that it was Mozart's Clarinet Concerto on tape that got her through the long sleepless nights of intense pain, biting back the sobs.

The relationship that eventually developed with Dubrovnik's remarkable, youthful Bishop Zelimir Puljic began quite unintentionally. Dubrovnik had produced many captains of sailing vessels over the centuries. They encountered serious storms at sea, and many, it seems, came to pledge that if God would bring them and their ship safely through this one, they would build a church or at least a votive chapel to commemorate the deliverance. This accounts in part for why such a small city, even a very Catholic city, should end up with sixty-six churches, in contrast to one synagogue, one Serbian Orthodox church and one mosque. There was no formal place of worship in the Protestant tradition, although we were conducting weekly studies on Wednesdays, with small, informal worship on Sunday mornings. We had begun in private homes and moved to a rented room in the Hotel Libertas beside our apartment.

Djuro worked at the Atlas tourist agency, and agreed to help me with language conversation. We often went fishing from the pier or elsewhere along the rocky shore, even from his boat. We also drank Turkish coffee together regularly at his house in the middle of town. Local radio broadcasts often provided the basis of discussion about vocabulary, sentence structure or just plain news. One day, in his kitchen, we heard the broadcaster announce a Muslim request for an additional place of worship.

"You need a place of worship for Protestants," Djuro said. I already knew that. "Many people come to Atlas asking where to find the Protestant church. We have to tell them there is none. You should ask the bishop for permission to use one of the churches." The idea seemed a fine one, but I didn't know the bishop.

"Then I'll ask for you."

We planned tentative inquiries with the bishop's secretary that might lead to an interview at the bishop's palace, just up the hill from our apartment. We agreed on a division of labour. Djuro would make the initial approach; I stayed on a pier by the Adriatic and prayed. Djuro and the bishop's secretary reached an agreement that this man Keith should write a letter outlining his request or proposal. The concept of seeking for such a place of worship was tested on the little core of believers with whom we regularly met for worship and Bible study. They considered it too improbable to be taken seriously.

"Maybe in Canada a bishop would consider this, but never in Yugoslavia." They had no objection in principle, just a solid conviction that it couldn't happen.

The letter was prepared. A date was set for a visit with Djuro to the palace. I wore the black homburg that I call my negotiating hat, and we were most courteously received, the first of what would become a series of visits. The bishop's opener was a real surprise.

"Where was your home in New Brunswick?" Definitely not a usual question. He informed me that he wasn't aware of Corn Hill, only of places like Fredericton, Saint John, Moncton and Sussex. He had served an apprenticeship at the Cathedral in Fredericton, New Brunswick. Bishop Puljic also added that he appreciated what he had seen of religious freedom in Canada, and desired the same for his country. Then we discussed my request for a place of worship. The outcome of the interview sounded like an excuse, like seeking a way out, but it was not.

"If it were up to me, yes. But each of our churches is controlled by one of the orders. I'd have to find an order that was willing to make one of their churches available to Baptists." That didn't sound very promising, and a number of weeks passed before any further word. Would there ever be further word? Before it came, we made that memorable trip to Vienna as the Gulf War opened, our turning point.

An invitation to visit the bishop again renewed our hope.

"I've found a church that will be available to you for your exclusive use, except on Christmas morning. We'll continue to hold mass once a year on Christmas morning, to keep the church in commission." This was splendid, but why not try for even more! I asked whether he would be available to bring greetings at the opening service, and he was willing to consult his calendar. When Palm Sunday was mentioned, he expressed regrets.

"I must absolutely be at the Dubrovnik Cathedral on Palm Sunday, but I'll send someone." That someone would turn out to be none less than Dr. Stanko Lasić, dean of the cathedral. It's just possible that Dr. Lasić's degree of enthusiasm didn't match that of his bishop, but he was there throughout our opening service, and brought his bishop's word of greeting. We had the key to what was called the Italian church, strategically located just off the Stradum in the centre of Dubrovnik. It seemed as though we had been given more—the key to Dubrovnik itself.

Visionary plans were considered, then prepared in detail. Our congregation would integrate into Dubrovnik's annual summer music program. The church's location and acoustics were superb. We made a number of contacts with people in the Dubrovnik symphony; in fact, a violin soloist was our immediate neighbour. We lacked only a musician and a concert piano.

Both were soon forthcoming. Voltr and Ursula Ivonoffsky fitted the calibre required. They taught music in Toronto as well as heading up the musical program at Blythwood Baptist Church. Voltr is a composer as well as conductor, and has been a guest conductor in both Vienna and Budapest. Ursula is a concert soloist. They were willing to set aside an entire year, something of a sabbatical. They would give daily recitals at noon in downtown Dubrovnik. I confessed to Voltr our lack of a piano; he thought he knew the solution.

We returned to Vienna in September of 1991 armed with the name and address of a representative of the Bösendorfer piano company. Appearing at their headquarters (wearing the black negotiating homburg hat, of course), I was received courteously by a man who gave me just over an hour as we went through our proposal for Dubrovnik. Yes, he would be prepared to make one of their concert grand pianos available for one year. Their own company vehicle would move the piano between Vienna and Dubrovnik, but of course I would need to pay the fuel costs both ways. No problem.

It turned out that this courteous man was the director himself. Little did I know how prized are those Bösendorfer pianos. One Canadian overstated it this way. "There are pianists who would kill for the privilege of playing regularly on a Bösendorfer." Somewhere here in our boxes of archives there rests a Bösendorfer folder, with all the details of a plan that never came to fruition. Within weeks of the negotiations at the Bösendorfer headquarters Dubrovnik was under siege and the Keiths were unable to return.

Our interim year away from Croatia represents the period of most intense fighting between Croatia and Serbia. We spent a few short weeks

During extensive church visits in Slovakia, translation was most often volunteered by Zuzka, who is a professional translator.

at the Fryckholms' empty home in Vienna, then moved to the village of Miloslavov just outside of Bratislava, in Slovakia.

The Keith interval at Miloslavov began in Czechoslovakia and ended in the Slovak Republic. We found ourselves in yet another country that was in breakup during our time of residence, but this one was peaceful. Our motivation for moving there may have been financial initially, but the warmth of reception and the degree of integration into the churches there left us with a sense of family acceptance and ties that will last a lifetime.

Much happened that year in Slovakia. The time came when it was appropriate to visit Croatia, just to keep in touch. Major conflict was underway between Serbia and Croatia, in several regions, but Zagreb seemed to be untouched. I called Dr. Branko Lovrec, president of the Baptist Union of Croatia, in Zagreb and asked him how best to get there. He implied that the only feasible way was by rail so I went to the station and bought a ticket, without consulting a map. That was my first mistake. The itinerary read like a news bulletin of the war zone in Croatia's Slavonia region. Vinkovci, Vukovar and Subotica were stations along the way. This prompted another call to Branko Lovrec, giving him his best laugh of the week.

Taking a ticket back for a refund is complicated under any circumstance but this ticket vendor, who obviously was not following news developments out of Croatia, could not be led to believe that the railway was closed in that region. I think she was saying, "Keep it until later when the line opens again." Not giving up that easily, my perseverance won through to a ninety percent refund—not bad under the circumstances.

Chalk up that other ten percent to my own lack of research and failure to know precisely what was needed. Travel from Bratislava to Vienna, then south through Graz in Austria and on through Slovenia to Zagreb was simple enough. I found Zagreb to be a city under siege.

While making preparations, it occurred to me to take a suitcase full of cured hams, salami, cheese and a few other products not requiring refrigeration but offering good food value. These were scarcely mentioned when I arrived, but were recited four years later as having been a major happening. There were indeed problems with food supplies, as with electricity. The city was blacked out at nights as a precaution against air raids. The presidential palace had been hit. Windows throughout the city were taped against blasts, and sandbagging was extensive. With apologies that homes were full, my hosts booked me into the Hotel Dubrovnik, on the main square at Zagreb. Not since Angola had I laid out everything so carefully before bedding down. Glasses, wallet, passport, clothing— all must be at the ready, within reach and easy to locate in the dark, in case of an air raid. There was none that night.

Dr. Branko Lovrec is a most versatile man. Having studied at Wheaton, Illinois, he is at home in the Western world, yet still totally at home in his own. He had laid aside his successful medical practice to found *Duhovna Stvarnost*, a Christian resource centre. His focus those days was on publications, but it would rapidly become humanitarian aid, at least on a temporary basis. His utter integrity, credibility and administrative gifts brought it all together. He held that prized combination of respect from within the country and from outside. Branko met me at the train and brought me up to date. He and I concluded that a visit together to Dubrovnik was strategically important, but it was not to happen during this Croatia visit in November 1991 when hostilities were running high.

Croatia was facing severe food crises, and we sent faxes from Zagreb to CBM's Sharing Way outlining the need. CBM took the initiative, sharing the cost with the Baptist World Alliance and other agencies, resulting in two hundred tonnes of wheat flour, one hundred tonnes of vegetable oil and two hundred and seventy-five tonnes of beans, secured through the Canadian Foodgrains Bank. Dr. Josip Mikulić played an innovative and constructive role. An executive with Croatia's national oil company, he arranged for their ships to pick up the food at a Canadian port. This represented a first in CBM's long experience with international relief.

The eventual visit to Dubrovnik with Branko Lovrec took place at the end of February 1992. The only way open to us was by ship. We went over the mountains to Rijeka by bus, shared a cabin on the coastal steamer, and were in Dubrovnik in less than twenty-four hours of overnight ship travel. The main siege of Dubrovnik was now past, but the devastations were scarcely cleaned up, let alone repaired. Small ships were lying on their sides at the bottom of the harbour; there were evidences of the naval bombardment, and signs of damage from mortars everywhere. Dubrovnik's famous luxury tourist hotels around Babin Kuk were obviously being put to other use. With refugees by the thousands converging from surrounding areas as well as from Bosnia, the terraced balconies, which resembled the bridge of a ship, mostly flew the flag of drying laundry.

The flag of Yugoslavia, now a hostile flag, flew over the castle on the hill above Dubrovnik, where Napoleon's troops had been stationed in the early nineteenth century. One did not linger long in certain exposed and perilous locations where sniper fire had been taking its toll. Branko and I stayed at Villa Milica, the apartment where Virginia and I had lived. Milica was an efficient and capable business person in whom we had not previously noted a lot of emotion. When I mentioned our prayers for her during the difficult days she dissolved in tears, and began listing the disasters that had occurred all around her while she and her house were spared. Neighbours on three sides were killed or wounded, and the Hotel Libertas across the road had been devastated by incendiary mortars. Milica's crowning revelation came as she took us down to see the metal door of the garage under her house. A mortar had come in at an angle, pierced the metal door but remained there on the floor of her garage, unexploded.

Branko worked closely with Milica's son, Dr. Robert Gvozdenović. Together they made arrangements for gifts of medical supplies for the new hospital, not even completed, that was treating many war victims. Well marked as a hospital, it had been a special target for deliberate bombardment. This happened in many places. Ambulances were also singled out as special targets.

Branko also arranged for supplies to Dubrovnik's soup kitchen.

We tried, unsuccessfully, to get assistance for an institution assisting the mentally challenged. During these days we spoke with many around Dubrovnik, including the conductor as well as the business manager of the symphony orchestra, hoping to keep alive our concept for the musical program, or at least further some international exchanges of musicians. We planned projects that never came to fruition. Looking at those efforts from a sports perspective, unless there are shots on goal there will be no scores. It is always exciting to show people under duress that practical Christian concern is many sided. It takes into consideration the whole person, including physical and cultural needs along with spiritual needs. Rarely are people reluctant to pray with someone whose interests take in all of their needs.

For three days and four nights Branko and I stayed in Dubrovnik, still surrounded and under siege. There was gunfire, the rattle of automatic weapons both light and heavy, always close and often intense. The fourth night was an exception and that is the only night I found it difficult to sleep. I remembered São Salvador under siege. The quiet nights were the dangerous ones in Angola, and it was on that quiet fourth night at Dubrovnik that I was most tense. Nothing dramatic happened, however, and on March 5 we departed on schedule.

Travelling among the beautiful islands of the Adriatic on our way out, Branko and I paced the deck and laid the plans that would bring us back to Croatia later in the year to establish residence at Varaždin north of Zagreb. At the time of that trip Dubrovnik's future was still unsettled. Our concern was to locate a relatively quiet corner of Croatia from which we could serve Eastern Europe. Language was one consideration. Having made beginnings in Croatian, there was a lot to be said for building on that foundation.

Communication was another consideration. During our year in Miloslavov, a country village located a half hour northeast of Bratislava, we had been operating on a shoestring—and very much in harmony with

Bratko Horvat (beard) and other Croatian Baptist leaders gather for a meal.

the local economy. However, we were in need of better communications facilities, including arrangements for travel. Phone service, although inexpensive, was inadequate and less than dependable. We were spending long hours on buses and trains. Taking the local bus at five to connect with a train to Vienna at six, to connect with a train to wherever we needed to be later loses its glamour after a while.

Following a short interval in Canada we returned in August 1992 to live at Varaždin, Croatia. This historic city and cultural centre had been recommended to us by Dr. Branko Lovrec who facilitated introductions to local leaders, notably Bratoljub Horvat, known to most as "Bratko," but also to Dr. Maršanić, a medical doctor and Bratko's father-in-law, and to Pastor Nikola Vukov. Due to the initiatives of very remarkable people, remarkable things had been taking place among Croatian Baptists, and continued to develop over the next four years and beyond.

Among the Baptist leaders in and around Varaždin and Čakovec, Bratko in particular displayed an ample vision, fierce dedication to Jesus as his Lord and a remarkable ability to make things happen. That does not necessarily make it easy for all Croatian colleagues to relate to him, cooperate with him or even to fully appreciate him. Bratko, with his brother and his sister, own and run an electronics business. All three were also very active in the local Baptist church. Bratko also functions as lay pastor of that congregation, which became our home base.

A notable feature of the small Baptist Union in Croatia is its multiethnic composition, both at the level of pastoral leadership and congregational makeup. The outstanding degree of ethnic integration drew much attention from the local communities and even from government officials. Few they were, these Croatian Baptists, yet they made an impact on the nation. Ethnic resentments ran strong in the community at large. The population was surprised and impressed to find that in these little Baptist congregations Serb, Croat, Bosnian and others were regularly praying and working together. One also found ethnic integration in the Pentecostal churches, they being the other main Protestant group in Croatia.

It is the grace of God that permits people, under the pressure of either nationalistic or patriotic propaganda to live above the prejudices expressed by their neighbours and their community, and to demonstrate in a practical way the love of Christ within that difficult context. It happens. I have seen it in many countries. It requires deliberate decisions and considerable personal discipline. It is the grace of God that can make a difference. That grace of God will be greatly needed and perhaps even severely tested in our Canada of the present and of the near future.

Three republics out of what had formerly been Yugoslavia were the main players in the political and military tensions as we experienced them from within Croatia. These were Serbia, Croatia and Bosnia. Each is multiethnic in varying degrees. Nationalistic fiction holds that all "true" Serbs are Serbian Orthodox by religion; churchmen and politicians both are happy to subscribe to this. A parallel nationalistic fiction has it that all "true" Croats are Roman Catholic. Around Varaždin there had once been a substantial component of Reformed churches following Luther's tradition, but they were erased by persecution. The Baptist denomination

The warehouse of Horvat Elektronika received and coordinated aid for refugees from all over Europe. A truck is loading for Bosnia from "Bratko's warehouse."

(as well as Pentecostals) proved to be something of an anomaly, for each congregation would be found to be multiethnic, including Croat, Serb, Romanian, Hungarian, Slovak, Czech and former Muslim as well.

Refugees in Croatia, having come from different areas and even from different republics of what had been the former Yugoslavia, tended to be stereotyped according to their conflicting ethnic communities. Even the dominant religions fortified those stereotypes. People assumed that each group kept essentially to itself, that each might be helped by interest groups assisting those of one religion or another, or by non-sectarian organizations like the United Nations or the Red Cross. Perhaps the most important feature of projects spearheaded by Baptists is that they were implemented without distinction of race or creed, based solely on need. When people found evidence of love and concern without bias, the concept seems to have been really surprising. A number of people remarked about it pointedly. It made a community impact. These were evidences

A Canadian contingent of United Nations troops patrols a street in Pakrac.

of the grace of God. We became involved in a number of such refugee assistance programs.

Truck drivers from all over Western Europe began to make an interesting discovery, and they spread the word among their colleagues. They discovered that if they could gather a load of goods to assist refugees, and drive it as far south as the *Horvat Elektronika* warehouse near Varaždin, they were assured of an intriguing experience. In fact it was probable that they would return home enthused to gather another load, and often with an additional truck driver or owner in tandem, bringing his added contributions as well.

Bratko is not a "control" person; he is a facilitator. When a driver showed up with help for refugees, Bratko's attention focused on how to help that person fulfil his or her goals in the most interesting and satisfying way.

"Would you like to distribute these things at the refugee camp?" "Would you prefer to drive this load to the town of Pakrac or to Karlovac?"

"Do you have a couple of extra days to do a run into Bosnia? If so, I'll send a guide with you." Others were only able to deliver their load of goods to the warehouse and then return home, due to their work responsibilities.

Some of the drivers had life-changing experiences themselves. I recollect my ride with a truck owner from Germany on the last day of 1992, when I served as his guide. On the way to Pakrac with his load of donations and then on the way back we talked of his family situation, a marriage in trouble. We discussed the implications of Christian faith, and of a life committed to the service of Jesus. When we got back, Bratko asked me to bring the message at their New Year's Eve service. This truck driver was among a half dozen that night who made Jesus Lord of their lives.

Extensive registries were established. Bratko engaged people to keep track of what assistance went where and in what quantities, aiming for some sort of equity in distribution. These operations, including registration and distribution, all tended to centre around his electronics warehouse, where teams of volunteers regularly sorted the various shipments that had been offloaded, making up family packets and stacking the resources according to categories. This warehouse, with its available floor space of well over 5,000 square feet, had an average turn-around time of about four days, full to empty to full again, in the busiest of seasons, which tended to be around Christmas and Easter.

The volunteer truck drivers proceeded to gather their loads of contributions in Europe, bringing whatever was available. One might come with five or ten tonnes of yogurt or butter that had only a few days before becoming stale-dated. Another would have second-hand mattresses, bed springs, old wood stoves and used clothing. There was great need for basics such as rice, flour, beans, sugar, and for toiletries such as soap, shampoo, toothpaste and the like.

Contributors included church groups, businesses, service groups, families, even communities. Bratko never knew at a given moment how many loads were on the way, when they would arrive, what country they were coming from, or what they might contain. When he woke up in the morning to look over toward his warehouse there might be two or more full-sized trucks with attached trailers, and an assortment of smaller vans. Someone with a different disposition could have been destroyed by the disorder and chaos this process produced. His family were as gracious as possible about the inevitable turmoil in home and business. There were certainly lots of family disruptions. Teams of volunteers camped in the basement of their home, and often ate at their table. Furthermore the family business had to absorb endless additional costs such as phone calls, heat and electricity, heavy transportation of goods to various distribution points, as well as the salaries of additional staff, printing costs and sundries.

The refugee population tended to be made up mostly of women with children, but with a smattering of men too old or infirm to fight. Their points of origin seemed to be about equally divided between Serbian-occupied areas of Croatia and the conflict zones of Bosnia-Herzegovina. The Croatian government had made available various army barracks around Varaždin to house refugees. The railway siding at Čakovec had a cluster of boxcars and railway work cars, each of which held two families. Many families had also been accepted into homes or had arranged to rent a room in a private house.

It soon became evident that refugee children needed special help if they were to gain admission to the Croatian school system, which would permit them to continue their education. Doing nothing would condemn them to a life on the streets, losing yet another year of schooling. The spin-off of no activity would lead to delinquency and the related social implications.

The first concrete needs we identified, studying their situation with Bratko and others, were for footwear, plus book bags and specified learning materials that were designated for each grade. These requirements were spelled out in precise detail, perhaps a carry-over from the Communist era. As long as they were able to turn up with the indicated materials the children would be admitted to the school system. No special tuition fees would be charged.

For each of the next four years Canadian Baptist Ministries approved the raising of special funds and the project went ahead. It turned out that needs were slightly different each year. We continued to support children from one year to the next, adding new participants and deleting those who moved. Some students we followed on into high school. Our oldest student from among those sponsored even proceeded on to university in Zagreb, and we helped with books for the first two years of his medical studies. Each year we were thanked with a flow of tears from parents expressing amazement that unknown friends half a world away were contributing funds to help their children pursue their education even in this time of war.

The specific requirements for workbooks and materials in each class called for extensive detail work; much of this was done by Shevko, a teacher from Brchko in northern Bosnia. Shevko and his family lived in one of the railway cars. We visited with them often, had them in our home, and became close friends with them.

An incident with Shevko and his family is just one example among many of the grace of God at work. Three visitors from the U.S.A. had come to Croatia to research and possibly design a cattle project. We were passing through Čakovec with them on our way back home after a day of visiting farms and institutions in the Croatian countryside. As we approached a certain intersection a conviction came to me that I should take them to pay a brief visit to some Bosnian refugee families living in the railway cars.

Having turned in that direction I had a few minutes to describe how these refugees were suddenly forced to leave their homes on such short notice that the teachers we would visit first actually had come away without their diplomas and certification for teaching. These are refugees with a difference, people accustomed to two salaries, their own home with appliances, their own vehicle and many other conveniences. They now shared life in a railway car with Raïf, whom they had not known previously, and had not chosen to live with.

That day's evidence of God's grace first showed itself in the timing of our arrival. A military vehicle was parked by the car where Shevko and

Assistance to refugee students included a pre-medical student from Bosnia. Proud parents were grateful.

Senaida lived; soldiers with automatic weapons were at their door. It seems that they had just arrived with orders to take Shevko away with them. We were not particularly welcomed by the military. That day I was glad to have been able to keep the Ontario registration plates on the car. They were a statement that international observers had arrived on the scene. I walked up and greeted Shevko, standing between soldiers who had just instructed him to get his coat and go with them. Shevko requested five minutes for coffee with his friends before leaving. His wife, Senaida, wringing her hands as she stood at the door of their railway car, turned to boil water on their little heater to make Turkish coffee.

The soldiers gave us black looks as we four crowded into the railway car with Shevko and Senaida. The time allotted was brief, and we knew it. The army waited outside. Senaida's hand trembled as she worked. With Shevko's departure she would have little or no hope of ever seeing him again. Would he be sent to the front to dig trenches? Would he become part of a "prisoner exchange"? Or would it be worse? As she served each of us our little cup of hot black coffee the cups literally danced on the saucers with the shaking of her hand. Words were few. There was no small talk.

My question as we finished coffee was not a new one to them.

"Would you like us to have prayer together?"

"Oh yes, please."

We stood in a tight circle, arms on each other's shoulders. We were three Americans, two Bosnians, one Canadian, and our Lord evidently present. The prayer was also short, committing Senaida and their two sons to his care, committing Shevko into the Lord's hands as he prepared to go with the soldiers. We visitors began to take our leave; what else could we do? I chose to give my calling card to the officer in charge, for no logical reason, commenting on my association with My Neighbour, the humanitarian organization Bratko Horvat directed locally. The officer didn't thank me for the card, but he did put it in his pocket. We deliberately took some photos, without asking permission – perhaps the most risky part of the whole intervention. With that we got into our vehicle and drove away, overcome with a sense of helplessness as we looked back at Shevko and Senaida among the soldiers.

Life was busy in those days and we had no phone connection with the railway cars. When it became possible to visit the siding for a follow-up visit my own faith had not prepared me for anything but the worst. Senaida came running this time, her greeting pouring out in a flood of tears.

During our relationship with Shevko and Senaida, I had classified Senaida as a reluctant person. She was very nervous, and Shevko had confided to me that she did not like to appear in public. Shevko, with sons Adil and Mohammed, had often attended our worship services at Puščine. Senaida had never been with them. I had her categorized as being probably less than enthusiastic about Shevko's consistent invitations for me to lead in prayer when we visited from time to time. In that I was wrong. This time her words were pouring out.

"Each time you prayed with us something happened."

I would not have been able to recount the various issues we had prayed about together. I was not keeping track, but Senaida was keeping her own scorecard.

"The first time you prayed for my family. I had not heard from them for two years. The next week I got a letter."

The second incident Senaida cited as an answer to prayer is one I can no longer recollect.

"Then you prayed with us about Raïf's son who had been lost for so long, and he came back."

Raïf's situation was certainly a sad one. His wife had been killed as the two of them tried to escape together across a river. His oldest son had been killed in a battle. This younger son, when we met him was a nervous wreck, and scarcely able to talk. He had received multiple wounds.

"Now you prayed for Shevko, *and they didn't even take him away.*"

My evaluation of what had been happening that day as we stood in a circle to pray was totally inadequate. I had assumed that only the three Americans and I were praying with expectation.

While interacting with Bratko at a number of levels, I was also working with Pastor Nikola Vukov on two or three projects. Together we visited extensively with families in the army barracks and the railway cars. This usually included drinking Turkish-style coffee, which can be hard on one's stomach when taken during visit after visit. We always heard the family's concerns, and normally ended our visit with prayer. Eight or ten people would often sit with us for the prayer time. Many of those would in turn join us at Sunday worship. As Nikola and I made our entrance to the army barracks it was not unusual to hear several windows opening, whether upstairs or down, and then shouted appeals to make sure we would include them in the day's visits.

My knowledge of Croatian was adequate for these visits, but I didn't have enough competence for public speaking. So I normally preached through a translator, preferably Ivica. Ivica Horvatić was a university student who had joined our weekly Bible studies and served as translator. When I was absent, if Nikola didn't lead the study Ivica might lead, based on notes I had shared with him. When I discovered that Ivica was travelling all the way from Zagreb by bus each week then returning to his studies the following morning, I offered to find someone else to translate, to save him the two hours' bus travel.

"But I don't want to miss the action." During our three years in Croatia Ivica's service as my translator served as something of an apprenticeship for him. Just before we left he was ordained as a deacon at the Puščine church with the right to conduct holy communion. One of the great disappointments of our time at Varaždin came when Nikola was no longer willing to interact with Bratko. The Bible studies we began in Varaždin now appear to have resulted in two distinct congregations, one of which has an outreach to another village nearby.

Bihać, in Bosnia-Herzegovina, made international headlines for months on end, under bombardment and constant sniper fire. On the tenth day after the siege had been lifted I went with Bratko and a truck delivering supplies. We brought 40,000 fresh eggs for the 850-bed hospital, fourteen tonnes of potatoes, two tonnes of honey (in steel drums), plus operating room linens, medicines, other hospital supplies and a few sundries.

While I sat in the hospital cafeteria, which once again had coffee to serve, I heard stories from hospital workers who pointed out that the table at which we sat had been in the direct line of fire of a sniper post. Harsh stories out of Bihać were already familiar to me from visits to the Life Centre, where I had met fifteen-year-old Edina, who had been standing beside her mother in this very hospital when her mother was struck down and killed by mortar shrapnel. Edina had taken over care of her little sisters Zurina, ten, and Indira, eight. All three of these children, like many other thousands, bear the deep emotional scars of family tragedy. Knowing the victims personally puts a much more solemn face on the casualties of war that so easily pass over our heads as we pay half attention to a newscast.

That day Bratko and I spent about an hour with the young military commander in army fatigues who was the mayor of Bihać. Adnan Alagić sat up very straight on hearing Bratko's question about what his city's most urgent needs would be.

"We are now free and we need nothing." That was the voice of relief and of pride speaking. Then he slumped down in his chair and added quietly, "But we have nothing, and we need everything." As the conversation proceeded, he chose to focus not on what was their greatest need, but what had been their greatest tragedy.

"Ten thousand children have lost three years of schooling—thirty thousand years of schooling lost." He still had teachers, he still had students, but the facilities had been destroyed and supplies were non-existent. Bratko then began with details on how he hoped to be able to change some of that.

Two other Canadian visitors had arrived that day. The mayor took us all on a tour of the suburb Gulabić, which had suffered such devastation. As I prepared to take a photo a sharp voice reminded me that I was not to step off the paved section, since the surroundings held an abundance of land mines. The land mine scourge will continue to claim its victims for decades to come.

There is no instrument with which to measure the inner destruction, the spiritual destruction that accompanies war, especially ethnic conflict among populations that have lived side by side. This dimension of destruction cannot be quantified. It is a fearful and highly destructive force, reaching beyond the grave, transmitted by one generation to the next. Yet, reconstruction is possible. Hope exists. We had the privilege of interacting with many different programs in Croatia, each of which integrated this component of spiritual hope, none of which forced religion upon people. What hope could there ever be in religion, when religion is at the heart of so much of the conflict? The hope, and the new way lies not in religion, but in a person, Jesus Christ, and in a relationship to God through him.

Perhaps not enough has been made of how refugees, while carrying so many memories—and such strong memories they are—of abuses and atrocities, have also tasted of the grace of God. Conversion experiences have permitted them to forgive, to love again, to become reconciled to former enemies, including those who had wronged them blatantly. I have seen no evidence that forgiveness of this nature and in this degree can be achieved through education, persuasion, propaganda or even logic. The forces of hatred and the natural inclination to secure revenge continue to escalate their upward spiral, often enhanced by politicians and the media. Change comes only when individuals and/or groups deliberately opt for patterns of emotion, behaviour and relationship that break the vicious cycle. It happens. When it happens it is a work of the Spirit of God. For decades I have believed that Jesus Christ is the hope of the twisted and vicious world in which we live. Never have I seen more striking or more convincing evidence than in our years in Eastern Europe, especially those while we were based in Croatia, from 1992 to 1995.

A pastor who must remain anonymous shared with me his conversation with a sobbing young soldier of the Serbian army. He and his colleagues had been forcibly recruited for military service. He spoke to my friend of their being sent on evening missions of "cleansing" in the eastern Slavonia area of Croatia that had recently been a battleground. Isolated farmhouses had been devastated, but civilian populations, especially women, children and the elderly, still sheltered in the basements of these gutted buildings. The nightly assignment of the patrols was to systematically visit these scattered and shattered remains. The patrols were to approach quietly and listen carefully for any indication of life or movement. Where there was a sound they were to throw in a grenade or two, then move on.

The realization of what he had been doing was utterly devastating to this young soldier. My friend spoke to him of God's forgiveness and of the availability of a different kind of "cleansing," a cleansing from personal sin, through faith in Jesus and the experience of the new birth. That experience of the new birth does not remove all the scars, but it makes healing possible. That young man, and others of similar experience, found freedom to accept themselves, to forgive others, to be reconciled, to love once again.

A popular saying has it that "the devil is in the details." Is it possible and practical to integrate conflicting ethnic entities into one worshipping church community, into one congregation? Again and again it was shown to be possible, practical, feasible.

On a Saturday afternoon at Pušćine, the symbolism of baptism by immersion took on a very special meaning for me. All nine of the baptismal candidates that afternoon had been driven from their homes by war. As they were invited to come forward for baptism, and were immersed under water—symbolizing their burial with Jesus to their former lives— the variety of their ethnic origins was striking. Vlado was first, an ethnic Croat. His wife Radojka was second, an ethnic Serb. The third was Mohammed, from what is called the Muslim community. The rest were equally of varied origins. Buried to what lay behind them, they were accepting a new oneness that involved love and reconciliation.

But what of the practicalities, the details? Anyone can stage-manage a production for show, but will it last beyond the door of the theatre? And even the church can become a theatre. The first affirming evidence surfaced hours later, during a chance encounter with two of them on the street. Vlado and Mohammed, buried to the animosities of their rival ethnic communities, were beginning to live out the friendship that would be seen day after day over the next two years, for as long as I remained in the area.

Naturally many of our programs focused on the immediate needs of refugees and other war victims, but other enterprises addressed longer-term development needs. One of these—another of Bratko's initiatives— was a cattle project. Having grown up working with cows, I loved the concept. In fact, I enjoyed working with this project much more than I ever remember enjoying getting up before dawn to milk cows by hand, from about the age of seven. This project developed the right way, starting with a locally recognized need. Actually, several factors converged to call for this cattle project.

First, hostilities had reduced the number of cattle so drastically that the country was no longer able to produce enough milk or meat for local consumption. Cattle had been deliberately killed and eaten. Cattle had been killed incidentally as war casualties, the meat wasted. Farmers had been killed. Farm families had been driven from their farming land and whole areas, mined, were no longer available for farming.

Second, there were people away from combat zones who had experience in handling cattle, people who had land excellent for crops and grazing. There were those who even had the necessary buildings. A wartime economy made it impossible for them to get enough of a financial start to increase their herds.

We set out to design a project that would meet needs for milk and its by-products, increase meat production, and help young families stay on the land and become more productive. Our resolve to help "little people" was questioned by government people several times, but in the end it was accepted and even lauded. The most efficient way to increase milk and meat production would have been to increase the herds of big operators. We chose instead to stay with a program that assisted dozens of families at a subsistence level.

The "we" with whom consultation took place involved Bratko, a group of local people with farming experience, representatives from the Ministry of Agriculture, and Southern Baptist friends who were prepared to share resources as well as experience and concepts. I recollect Tom Prevost as an essential early catalyst; and it was Tom who brought in key consultants from the state of Virginia. Bill Steele admitted no experience with cattle, but was willing to work hard at the administrative and committee work, making sure the financing for phase one was in place.

The visit of a Virginia cattleman and his colleagues, the "aggie" professor and the veterinarian, helped to bring it together. These men totally reversed our original concept of introducing new breeds, new stock, perhaps even new technology in terms of embryo implants. We drove through the countryside together, studying what was available, what needed to be imported. We visited farms, large and small. We toured the government breeding station. We consulted the meat-packing industry.

I think it is fair to say they were stunned by one particular experience. The cattleman and the professor were standing in front of a pen of registered, purebred Simmental heifers that were about to be shipped to the packing plant for *meat*. High-quality breeding stock like this would be

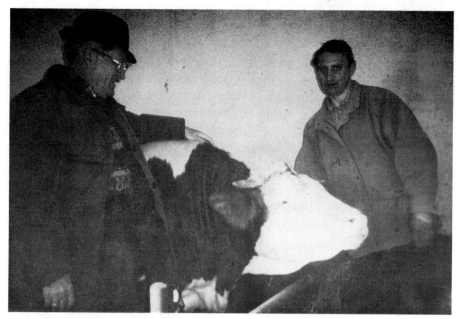

The Croatian cattle project helped small landowners replenish stock depleted by war.

available to us for the price of beef! Why would one consider importing stock when these conditions prevailed? The missing component was the funding to get the project underway, and the collective initiative of appropriate people to make the plan work with integrity.

We made it work, and it was a joy to be part of the eventual selection, distribution and full implementation. When I later learned that further phases of the plan were being implemented, and that assistance was reaching on into Bosnia, I received the information as comfortable confirmation of the process we had begun.

However, I look back at my last Friday morning in Croatia as perhaps the most solid unsolicited testimonial from outsiders. I was in the process of closing down our apartment permanently. Virginia was already back in Canada for health reasons. I had more than enough to do, but I had long ago learned that if Bratko called requesting my presence, it was never a waste of time. So I jumped in the car and made my way to the office beside his warehouse. He had three surprise visitors, representatives of the World Bank organization.

"We don't know what your cattle project is," they said, "but we were informed by the Ministry of Agriculture in Zagreb that it's the best development project in the country, so we had to come and talk with you."

In the end, it is not a word from bureaucrats that is the final seal of approval. Through this cattle project we developed an entirely new set of relationships. There were even those who came to personal faith through the process, especially through their contacts with Vlado Lesar, who visited the home of each family that received a cow, on at least three separate occasions.

Some of Bratko's spontaneous new projects led to amazing, long-term spin-offs in other directions. On one occasion he had invited me to address a gathering of teachers from Čakovec district. They were feeling both deprived and neglected in an economy that was suffering wartime inflation, and where they had few resources. Bratko asked whether it would be of help to them if we were to bring professional educators from Canada to conduct seminars in which there would be input as well as interaction. This met with an immediate and enthusiastic response. Six retired Canadian educators responded, five from British Columbia and one from Nova Scotia. The seminars were a complete success.

After the seminars we introduced the Canadian participants to another cluster of operations of the Baptist Union of Croatia. The Life Centre, Peace Centre and Hope Centre are a trio of rehabilitation ministries situated on the Adriatic coast at Crikvenica, and developed through the vision and energies of Pastor Stevo Dereta. Direct involvement by Canadian Baptist Volunteers in these programs stems from the educators' seminars.

The Life Centre has specialized in bringing in groups of up to fifty refugees at a time, providing ten days of physical and spiritual refreshment in a congenial context beside the Adriatic. People deprived of home and possessions, their recent history having centred around refugee camps and deprivation, deeply appreciate clean sheets, lace curtains, tablecloths and nutritious food, especially when served up in a peaceful environ-

Ray Slade (and his wife, Edna-May, not shown) were the moving force behind teams of volunteers helping renovate the Hope Centre.

ment where they may even learn to smile again, to sing and even to pray. They speak of being given loving care, of being treated with dignity, of receiving an infusion of hope, and of becoming human once again.

The Life Centre functions in an old hotel that has been refurbished by volunteer assistance using donated materials from Austria, Switzerland, Germany, England, Wales and Sweden, with more recent contributions from Canada and the U.S.A. Volunteer assistance is involved in running the institution, which would not have sufficient income to hire all the staff needed, though there is an efficient, capable and dedicated Croatian staff at the heart of its ministry—Stevo and his team.

The Peace Centre has its focus on ministry to refugee children from Bosnia. Located on the beach just south of the Life Centre and virtually in sight of it, this second institution is located in an old villa. Children deprived of their childhood, who have spent far too much time in bomb shelters and bombarded apartments, get a chance to enjoy sunshine, fresh air and the waterfront for up to five weeks at a time. They receive professional psychiatric care from Croatians drawn to this ministry.

The Hope Centre, established last, is still developing. It is located on the other side of the mountains and away from the ocean in an old, three-storey factory that is still under reconstruction – by volunteers and with donated materials, of course. Canadian Baptist volunteer teams contribute to it periodically, the initiative being sparked by Ray and Edna-May Slade of First Baptist Church, Vancouver, who were introduced to Crikvenica at the end of their participation in the educators' seminars. The Hope Centre has been established primarily for the vocational rehabilitation of amputees and other wounded, but will probably affect a wider clientele.

The story of our Croatian experience is really a story of relationships that developed with outstanding people, remarkable people. One of those was certainly Dr. Branko Lovrec. Branko was always there for consultation when major decisions were needed, and we became close friends. He made a profound impact through meeting the needs of the suffering in Bosnia before other organizations got into those activities. He and his colleagues virtually wrote the book on accountability and reporting on resources donated, exemplary in every way. When organizations such as Samaritan's Purse of the U.S.A. or Tear Fund of the U.K. advertise their programs as developed in Croatia and Bosnia, it may not be immediately evident that those are really the programs developed by Dr. Branko Lovrec and colleagues, toward which these organizations provide resources.

Ladislav and Melanija Ružička of Karlovac became special friends. He is pastor of the Baptist congregation at Karlovac, and for the three years that we lived at Varaždin this young couple lived on the fringe of war, in one of the areas where there were often "incidents." Melanija and Ladislav chose not to flee at the height of hostilities in 1991 when a tank battle raged around their house. On one day they lay flat on the floor of their apartment during the height of battle, then picked up about fifty pieces of shrapnel inside their rooms. Of course all their windows were blown out, and they spent much of the winter with only sheet plastic to shut out the wind and snow.

At age 103, Baptist pioneer, Jovo Jekić is interviewed by Dr. Branko Lovrec, president of the Baptist Union of Croatia. Jovo's daughter Ankica listens in.

From time to time, over those three years we lived in a Croatia that was at war, we visited combat zones, but only when they were reported to be relatively quiet. We had made a deliberate decision not to expose ourselves unnecessarily to hostile situations. The occasional visits would be to take supplies to posts where relief was being distributed, or to bring a word of encouragement and solidarity to those who chose to stay even through the heat of battle. Pakrac was one such place, and the Karlović family, who served the church and the distribution post there, are certainly among my personal heroes. Having been deliberately victimized, the father wounded seven times by bayonets, they still chose to live there in a perilous situation, ministering to all without distinction of race and creed.

Occasionally we were warned by United Nations observers to remove ourselves quickly from some area where they knew we were being observed through snipers' telescopes. By the grace of God we were kept safe through months of exposure to uncertain situations. It was a great reward to be assured time and again that our simple presence, regardless of whether or not we were able to contribute material assistance, made a positive difference in people's lives.

Looking back over a lifetime of transitions, the December departure from Croatia in 1995 was one of the very moving ones. On the final Sunday morning I was to preach at the Baptist church in Puščine, there would be a farewell meal at the home of Dr. Maršanić with a number of our closest friends, then I would drive across Slovenia and Austria, with Hamburg, Germany, as my destination. There would be final meetings relating to Albania, and I would deposit my car at the dock in Bremerhaven for shipment to Halifax. Mrs. Maršanić had prepared no less than two trays of her apple and cherry strudel with walnuts to see me through the trip.

Things proceeded as planned, but with a quiet surprise as I was taken aside by an acquaintance. He had been a military man, imprisoned toward the end of that career with a number of others who were rebelling against communism. He had spent eleven years in prison, and among his fellow prisoners was Franjo Tudjman, the first president of Croatia. In 1990 the government of Croatia had gathered together these former prisoners and honoured them as precursors of democracy. There in a corner of the dining room this friend removed from his lapel the gold pin he had been awarded.

"I want you to have this, because of the way you have related to my people," he said.

An acquaintance in Canada later asked me, "How could you accept something that had cost him so much?" My studied response is this: "How could I refuse a gift that cost so much?"

Epilogue

These chapters have been drawn together from our home base at Clear Lake, Ontario, conveniently located between Toronto and Ottawa. In addition to being a beautiful spot on water where family can gather, the location makes it quite feasible to pursue in retirement a portfolio entitled "Diplomatic Liaison" on behalf of Canadian Baptist Ministries.

Continuing evidences of the grace of God at work seem to surface with regularity as we pursue the various concerns relating to this portfolio. Within the past month those interests have involved working successfully with the Angolan Embassy in Ottawa to acquire residence visas so that others may serve in the country where we ourselves began.

Then, just yesterday, the process of finishing the writing of this book was interrupted by the need to continue interaction with Canada's Department of Foreign Affairs in the effort to reopen the private airports in the Democratic Republic of the Congo that President Kabila has closed in his attempt to restrict the flow of illicit arms. When private airports are closed, and when Mission Aviation Fellowship cannot move people and supplies, personnel working in the most remote of areas can no longer function effectively.

The communications systems now available, even to people in retirement, give access in a multitude of ways to all the nations. It is indeed interesting to note that "what goes around comes around" as these recent involvements again connected us to the first two countries in which we served overseas following language study. Beyond Angola and Congo, who can predict how many additional chapters of experience may yet be forthcoming, even in retirement!

It was a sense of God's call to obey the commission Jesus gave to his followers that first turned me from a career in banking to pursue fulfilment of the world mission of the church. That sense of direction, compulsion, leading, continues strong.

Make disciples in all the nations.

This book carries numerous accounts of trauma, but violence and pain must not have the final word. The accent must fall on the grace of God, which is without measure. When called upon it proves to be sufficient in every time of need. During the course of writing this book, these few lines from a gospel song repeatedly ran across my memory, sometimes audibly, sometimes silently:

> His love has no limits,
> His grace has no measure,
> His power has no boundaries known unto man,
> For out of his infinite riches in Jesus
> He giveth, and giveth, and giveth again.